AIRCRAFT STRUCTURAL MAINTENANCE
Student Workbook
THIRD EDITION

Production Staff
Lead Illustrator Amy Siever
Designer/Photographer Dustin Blyer
Designer/Production Coordinator Roberta Byerly

© Copyright 2005, 2008, 2009, 2013 by
Avotek Information Resources, LLC.
All Rights Reserved

International Standard Book Number 1-933189-33-9
ISBN 13: 978-1-933189-33-8
Order # T-AFSTR-0302

For Sale by: Avotek
A Select Aerospace Industries Inc. company

Mail to:
P.O. Box 219
Weyers Cave, Virginia 24486
USA

Ship to:
200 Packaging Drive
Weyers Cave, Virginia 24486
USA

Toll Free: 1-800-828-6835
Telephone: 1-540-234-9090
Fax: 1-540-234-9399

Third Edition
First Printing
Printed in the USA

www.avotek.com

Contents

To the Student — iv

1. Helicopter Fundamentals — 1
2. Fabric Covering — 13
3. Materials and Processes — 21
4. Airframe Metallic Structures — 35
5. Airframe Nonmetallic Structures — 43
6. Welding Techniques — 51
7. Painting and Refinishing — 63
8. Assembly and Rigging — 73

To the Student

This Student Workbook accompanies Introduction to Aircraft Maintenance, the first in a four book series created and published by Avotek. This workbook should be utilized as a tool for highlighting the strengths as well as pinpointing the weaknesses of the AMT student gathering the skill and knowledge necessary to build a strong foundation in the aircraft maintenance field. Specifically, it evaluates the progress made in applicable subject areas.

The foundation on which this workbook has been built assumes that the student is actively engaged in preparing for two goals: the first is to pass all required testing for the FAA Airframe and Powerplant Mechanic Certificate, and the second is to obtain the necessary skills and knowledge to function as an entry-level mechanic in the field. Both goals must be kept in mind and the material presented here has been designed to maintain that balance.

Each chapter of the text is divided into three different question formats and printed on perforated sheets for removal and presentation. They are presented as follows:

Fill in the Blank
These questions are designed to help the student understand new terminology and fundamental facts essential to the understanding of section material.

Multiple Choice
These questions offer a broader overview of the material by offering several possible answers, and allowing the student to identify the correct answer either through recognition or through the process of elimination.

Analysis
These are complex questions that require the student to access information presented in the text, analyze the data, and record a response. Successful completion of the analysis questions shows the student has a thorough understanding of the material contained in the chapter.

The answers for each set of questions are available from your course instructor.

Avotek® Aircraft Maintenance Series
Introduction to Aircraft Maintenance
Aircraft Structural Maintenance
Aircraft System Maintenance
Aircraft Powerplant Maintenance

Avotek® Aircraft Avionics Series
Avionics: Fundamentals of Aircraft Electronics
Avionics: Beyond the AET
Avionics: Systems and Troubleshooting

Other Books by Avotek®
Aircraft Corrosion Control Guide
Aircraft Structural Technician
Aircraft Turbine Engines
Aircraft Wiring & Electrical Installation
AMT Reference Handbook
Avotek Aeronautical Dictionary
Fundamentals of Modern Aviation
Light Sport Aircraft Inspection Procedures

Chapter 1
Helicopter Fundamentals

FILL IN THE BLANK QUESTIONS

name:

date:

1. The _____ was the first mass-produced helicopter.

2. Powered vertical flight was not possible until the basic concept of _____ was conceived and solved.

3. Rotation for the rotary wing on an autogyro is provided by the _____ .

4. The primary aft control on a helicopter is the _____ .

5. The major function of the answer in Question 4 is to overcome _____ and provide a means of controlling the _____ .

6. Most helicopter rotors use a _____ airfoil.

7. A relative wind striking the leading edge of the airfoil in Question 6 head-on will produce _____ ; therefore, this airfoil must have a/an _____ .

8. An airfoil with a _____ surface produces more lift than an airfoil with a _____ surface.

9. In helicopters, torque is applied in a _____ rather than a _____ plane.

10. Because of _____ , a force applied against a rotating body will take effect 90° later, in the direction of _____ .

11. An out-of-balance rotor blade on a helicopter causes a _____ vibration, or a/an _____ movement.

12. An out-of-track rotor blade on a helicopter causes a _____ vibration or a/an _____ movement.

13. A high-speed moving part that has been torqued incorrectly can cause a/an _____ vibration.

14. The answer to Question 13 will be evident by a _____ and a _____ .

15. Rotor tracking systems have focused on providing information that can be used to adjust the _____ to make the blades fly perfectly.

16. Maintenance technicians should know the capabilities of each method of NDI and know that no NDI method should ever be considered _____ by itself.

Chapter 1
Helicopter Fundamentals

FILL IN THE BLANK QUESTIONS

name:

date:

17. When talking about rotor systems, one important fact to remember is that not all helicopter rotors _____ .

18. When applied to rotor blades, the thrust-bending force that acts on propellers is called _____ .

19. If the speed of the blade on the advancing half of the rotor is the same as the speed on the retreating half, there is _____ of lift.

20. _____ of lift is created by forward movement of the helicopter.

21. Blade movement called _____ and _____ is necessary for an articulated rotor system to be aerodynamically balanced.

22. The spanwise axis about which a rotor blade rotates to change pitch is known as the _____ .

23. When the main rotor angle of attack and engine power are adjusted so that _____ equals _____ , the helicopter will hover.

24. When the angle of attack of both blades is increased equally while blade speed remains constant, the helicopter will _____ .

25. _____ is an out-of-balance condition in the rotor system of a helicopter on the ground that rapidly increases in frequency until the helicopter shakes itself apart. The emergency action is to _____ .

26. Helicopters designed to use one main and tail rotor system are referred to as _____ helicopters.

27. Because there is no anti-torque rotor, a _____ helicopter can apply full engine power to load lifting.

28. The rotor design concept that attempts to get around the speed limitations of the conventional helicopter is the _____ .

29. In flight maneuvers, movement around the lateral axis produces a nose-up or nose-down attitude, or _____ , which is accomplished by moving the _____ fore and aft.

30. In flight maneuvers, movement around the vertical axis produces a change in direction to the right or left called _____ , and is controlled by the _____ .

Chapter 1
Helicopter Fundamentals

FILL IN THE BLANK QUESTIONS

name:

date:

31. In flight maneuvers, movement around the longitudinal axis is called _____, produces a tilt to the right or left, and is accomplished by moving the _____ to the right or left.

32. The change from hovering to flying is called _____ and is done by moving the _____ forward.

33. If there is a key component that makes controlled helicopter flight possible, it is the _____ .

34. In single-rotor helicopters, torque is counteracted by the _____ .

35. When a helicopter is in a hover, it is affected by a process known as the _____ . You can tell if a pilot is compensating for this because the helicopter will hover with the _____ low.

36. In tandem-rotor, coaxial, and synchropter designs, the main rotors _____ , thereby neutralizing or eliminating torque.

37. _____ is achieved when the center of gravity, center of pressure, and blade-feathering axis all act at the same point.

38. Wooden rotor blades have a stainless steel leading edge attached to reduce _____.

39. The blade _____ is the shape of the rotor blade when viewed from above.

40. For the edge to work efficiently, airfoils must have a _____ edge that is thicker than the _____ edge.

41. The _____ edge is strengthened to resist damage, which happens most often during ground handling.

42. The main supporting part of a rotor blade is the _____ .

43. The answer in Question 42 always extends along the _____ of the blade.

44. The high-pressure side of the blade is the _____ and it is always painted a _____ to prevent glare into crew compartments during flight.

45. The surface area where two objects are bonded together is called the _____ .

46. A cheap method used to align rotor blades on the same plane of rotation is the use of _____ .

Chapter 1
Helicopter Fundamentals

FILL IN THE BLANK QUESTIONS

name:

date:

47. Aligning fully articulated tail-rotor blades an equal distance to one another with a 2° angle of lead to the blades is called _____ and must be done before they are _____ .

48. Even with engine failure, the rotor will still be turning the transmission and the pilot will still have _____ flight controls.

Chapter 1
Helicopter Fundamentals

MULTIPLE CHOICE QUESTIONS

name:

date:

1. Which of these paved the way for powered rotary-wing aircraft to fly successfully?
   a. Autogyros
   b. Flapping hinge
   c. Advancing rotor blades
   d. Hovering capability

2. The first licensed commercial helicopter was produced by:
   a. Sikorsky
   b. Cierva
   c. Bell
   d. Focke-Wulf

3. On a helicopter, which of these is supplied by the main rotor blades?
   a. Thrust
   b. Both drag and lift
   c. Lift
   d. Both thrust and lift

4. Which of these airfoils does not work well for helicopter rotors because of a shift in the aerodynamic center of pressure?
   a. Negative camber
   b. Top camber
   c. Zero camber
   d. Upper camber

5. Which of these is not a factor in how much lift an airfoil can develop?
   a. Air density
   b. Blade material
   c. Area
   d. Speed

6. Which of these is the point at which burbling takes place?
   a. Angle of incidence
   b. Critical angle of attack
   c. Critical angle of incidence
   d. Angle of attack

7. Why are high-altitude rescue operations with helicopters extremely difficult?
   a. Low density air reduces lift.
   b. Angle of attack increases the creation of eddies.
   c. Angle of incidence decreases, causing a stall.
   d. Rotor speed must increase to compensate for less relative wind.

8. What remains in one position at all angles of attack?
   a. The center of pressure of an unsymmetrical airfoil
   b. The airfoil chord line
   c. The center of pressure of a symmetrical airfoil
   d. The aerodynamic center of an airfoil

9. Each time the helicopter lifts off the ground, the transmission mount/mast tube is subjected to what type of stress?
   a. Torsion
   b. Bending
   c. Compression
   d. Tension

10. What type of stress is the same transmission mount/mast tube subjected to when it lands?
    a. Torsion
    b. Bending
    c. Compression
    d. Tension

Chapter 1
Helicopter Fundamentals

MULTIPLE CHOICE QUESTIONS

name:

date:

11. Which force tends to pull a component apart?
    a. Shear
    b. Strain
    c. Vibration
    d. Torsion

12. Which of these causes crystallization of metal, which can lead to mechanical failure?
    a. Torsion
    b. Strain
    c. High-frequency vibration
    d. Vibration absorbers

13. Any buildup of dirt, grease or fluid on or inside a high-speed part can cause:
    a. Harmonic vibrations
    b. An out-of-torque condition
    c. Shear
    d. High-frequency vibrations

14. Which type of rotor tracking system requires significant operator skill and training?
    a. Strobe-light tracking
    b. Flag tracking
    c. Electro-optical tracking
    d. Dynamic Solutions Systems optical tracker

15. Which of these methods of rotor-smoothing requires hundreds of flights to develop a single-flight program for a particular aircraft?
    a. Complex algorithm
    b. Improved fault-tolerant algorithm
    c. Bubble balancing algorithm
    d. Single-flight computer-based rotor-smoothing algorithm

16. On most rotor blades, which of these is determined by design and is not adjustable?
    a. Angle of incidence
    b. Rotor track
    c. Blade pitch
    d. Amount of centrifugal force

17. What is the circle formed by the rotating rotor blades called?
    a. Plane of rotation
    b. Axis of rotation
    c. Center of rotation
    d. Disc area

18. What permits the rotor disc to tilt, providing directional control in flight?
    a. Articulated rotor head
    b. Flapping
    c. Leading blade
    d. Lagging blade

19. Which of these creates a condition of unbalance with resulting vibration?
    a. Articulated rotor head
    b. Blade-flapping
    c. Leading blade
    d. Lagging blade

20. Which of these prevents the vibration referred to in Question 19?
    a. Articulated hub with dampers
    b. Semi-rigid hub with flap-stop
    c. Drag hinge and dampers
    d. Built-in droop stop

Chapter 1
Helicopter Fundamentals

MULTIPLE CHOICE QUESTIONS

name:

date:

21. The upward flexing of a rotor blade due to lift forces acting on it is called:
    a. Coning
    b. Blade flapping
    c. Hunting
    d. Drooping

22. The horizontal movement of the blades around a vertical pin is called:
    a. Coning
    b. Blade flapping
    c. Hunting
    d. Drooping

23. Which is a benefit of helicopter operations within ground effect?
    a. Hovering
    b. Lift-gravity balance
    c. Pitch control
    d. Reduction of power requirements

24. Which of the following remains a big concern for anyone who flies a helicopter with a fully articulated rotor system?
    a. Ground resonance
    b. Lower blade angle of attack
    c. Reduction of the rotor-tip vortex
    d. Hunting

25. Which of the following is usually caused by a hard ground contact and is more likely in aircraft with improperly maintained landing gear?
    a. Drooping
    b. Lift-gravity imbalance
    c. Dissymmetry of lift
    d. Ground resonance

26. Which of the following is a disadvantage of a tandem-rotor helicopter?
    a. Longitudinal instability
    b. More drag due to its shape and additional weight
    c. A smaller center-of-gravity range
    d. A retreating blade which can stall

27. With which one of these rotor systems can the blades be rotated to vertical once in flight?
    a. Single rotor
    b. Coaxial rotor blades
    c. Tiltrotor
    d. Synchropter

28. Which of these rotor systems has both rotors on the same mast, turning in different directions?
    a. Tandem
    b. Coaxial
    c. Tiltrotor
    d. Synchropter

29. Which type of rotor system has undesirable control problems in autorotation and almost always has a rudder and vertical fin to allow autorotation control?
    a. Tandem
    b. Coaxial
    c. Tiltrotor
    d. Synchropter

30. To change the angle of attack of the blades, move the:
    a. Directional control pedals
    b. Collective pitch control
    c. Cyclic control stick
    d. Swashplate

Chapter 1
Helicopter Fundamentals

MULTIPLE CHOICE QUESTIONS

name:

date:

31. Which of these are used in coordination to regulate the airspeed?
    a. Collective pitch control and cyclic pitch control
    b. Collective pitch control and directional control pedals
    c. Throttle and collective pitch control
    d. Cyclic pitch control and throttle

32. On turbine engine helicopters, what is the collective pitch stick synchronized with?
    a. Throttle
    b. Cyclic pitch control
    c. Carburetor
    d. Fuel control unit

33. Which of these twists or flexes to allow proper movement in a rotor system?
    a. Elastomeric bearings
    b. Articulated heads
    c. Adjustable drag braces
    d. Flapping hinges

34. Blades that can lead and lag individually during rotation are characteristic of which type of tail rotor hub?
    a. Flex-beamed type
    b. Hinge-mounted type
    c. Fully articulated type
    d. Fenestron tail rotor

35. Which of these tail rotor types is safer both on the ground and in flight because of a fan shroud?
    a. NOTAR
    b. Fenestron
    c. Fully articulated
    d. Coanda

36. Which of these stops accidents from tail rotor strikes by eliminating the tail rotor altogether?
    a. NOTAR
    b. Fenestron
    c. Flex-beamed
    d. Coanda

37. Which part of the blade is the section nearest the center of rotation that provides a means of attachment to the rotor head, and is heavier and thicker to resist centrifugal forces?
    a. Tip
    b. Spar
    c. Root
    d. Chord

38. Which part of the blade is furthest from the center of rotation and travels at the highest speed?
    a. Tip
    b. Spar
    c. Root
    d. Chord

39. To get more even distribution from lift, most rotor blades are:
    a. Weighted with balances
    b. Twisted positively from root to tip
    c. Twisted negatively from root to tip
    d. Tapered

40. In blade repair, damages are often located and classified according to:
    a. Their relation to the span line
    b. Their distance from the rotor head
    c. Their relation to the chord line
    d. Their distance from the tip

41. Which of these refers to the rotor blade width measured at the widest point?
    a. Span
    b. Planform
    c. Chord
    d. Root

42. Which of these is used as a reference line to make angular measurements?
    a. Leading edge, root to tip
    b. Trailing edge, root to tip
    c. Chord line
    d. Span line

43. Which type of weight used to balance the blades is the technician allowed to add, remove or shift?
    a. Tracking weights
    b. Spanwise balance weights
    c. Mass chordwise balance weights
    d. The technician is not allowed to move any of the above

44. Which type of weight change is computed mathematically when moving it is permitted?
    a. Tracking weights
    b. Spanwise balance weights
    c. Mass balance weights
    d. All of the above require calculations to compute the new center of gravity

45. Allowing the main rotor to rotate of its own free will, regardless of engine speed, is the:
    a. Free-wheeling unit
    b. Sprag clutch
    c. Torque effect
    d. Autogyro principle

46. Which of these will allow the engine to drive the rotors, but will not allow the rotors to turn the engine?
    a. Autorotor
    b. Torque effect
    c. Free-wheeling unit
    d. Sprocket clutch

47. Which of these describes the aircraft's tendency to rotate in the opposite direction to the main rotor, and the reason a tail-rotor is needed?
    a. Newton's First Law of Motion
    b. Torque effect
    c. Free-wheeling
    d. Autogyro principle

48. Which of these can a helicopter do that a fixed-wing aircraft cannot?
    a. Land without engine power
    b. Land with reverse thrust
    c. Land with zero forward speed
    d. Control speed of descent

Chapter 1
Helicopter Fundamentals

MULTIPLE CHOICE QUESTIONS

name:

date:

Chapter 1
Helicopter Fundamentals

ANALYSIS
QUESTIONS

name:

date:

1. Identify the primary difference between an autogyro and a conventional helicopter.

2. Why does a helicopter require more power to hover in ground effect at 7,000 feet msl than at sea level?

3. Name three reasons to balance rotor blades.

4. The primary advantages of helicopters are their ability to hover, land and take off vertically, and maneuver in close quarters. Based on your study of this chapter, what are some of the helicopter's disadvantages?

5. What techniques are used to compensate for a rotor blade's uneven lift characteristics during flight?

6. Identify three types of stress acting on a rotor blade and hub.

7. A helicopter's disc area and disc loading correspond to a fixed-wing aircraft's wing area and wing loading (pounds of aircraft weight per square foot of disc or wing area). How are the aerodynamic loads applied to each airfoil different?

8. On a fixed-wing aircraft, flight loads are transferred from the wing to the fuselage through the spar and carry-through structure. What component performs this function on a helicopter, and what level of stress does it carry?

9. On a fully articulated rotor system, what job do blade feathering, lead-lag, and flapping perform?

Chapter 1
Helicopter Fundamentals

ANALYSIS QUESTIONS

name:

date:

10. What are some of the disadvantages of the fully articulated rotor system?

11. What advantages are gained by employing rigid or semi-rigid rotor head systems?

Chapter 2
Fabric Covering

FILL IN THE BLANK QUESTIONS

name:

date:

1. In 1916, manufacturers began to use a compound of cellulose dissolved in nitric acid, referred to as _____, to help linen fabric covering the structures of planes retain its _____.

2. The transparent quality of the compound in Question 1 did nothing to protect the fabric from _____.

3. Around World War II, _____ became the covering material of choice for higher performance aircraft, eventually replacing textile fabric as the covering standard.

4. The _____ is the direction of threads along the length of the fabric.

5. When contrasting colors of fabric are used on an aircraft, the fabric will deteriorate more rapidly under the _____ because of the increased _____, which promote the growth of _____.

6. Before covering or recovering an aircraft structure, most FSDOs insist on a _____.

7. On the structure to be covered, all parts of a wooden structure should be inspected for _____ and areas made of metal should be checked for _____, _____, and _____.

8. Loosening and tightening _____ and _____ will bring wing spars into correct lateral alignment, and they should be secured to prevent _____.

9. To protect the fabric from the structural material, any tube ends or ends of other structural members that will come into contact with the fabric must be _____.

10. Once the first coat of dope has been applied, _____ should be done immediately.

11. Before beginning the covering process one item that is standard procedure is a _____ for the fuselage.

12. _____ is the covering method employed on all antique aircraft.

13. Due to the strength, durability and ease of covering, most aircraft owners are opting for _____ rather than the answer in Question 12.

14. The _____ is the only FAA-approved hand-sewn seam.

15. _____ tape should be applied over all lacing, seams, and all places where it is necessary or desirable to provide reinforcement, but not until the first coat of dope has dried.

Chapter 2
Fabric Covering

FILL IN THE BLANK QUESTIONS

name:

date:

16. All thread for hand sewing and cord for rib lacing must be coated thoroughly with _____ before use.

17. Whenever covering fabric is laced to any part of a structure, _____ tape is placed over the fabric along the underlying member, under all lacing.

18. _____ are installed in fabric surfaces to provide reinforcements around drainage and ventilation holes.

19. Both _____ and _____ dopes are the acceptable mediums for encapsulating the fibers of aircraft covering, but a tautening _____ dope is used on _____ .

20. The main advantage of using _____ dope is its fire resistance, but it does not have the _____ ability.

21. The main purpose of dope is to _____ and to produce a _____ .

22. The _____ of the fabric produces an increase in strength that allows the fabric to withstand the heavy air loads.

23. The answer in Question 22 also provides an almost _____ surface that protects the wing and fuselage structure from the damage of _____ .

24. As a major part of any re-cover, spacing of _____ is important to airworthiness, and you can verify original spacing by using an airplane's _____ chart.

25. Always put the starting knot on the _____ surface, never on _____ .

26. _____ is the greatest factor in the deterioration of dope and fabric, and _____ is added to the last few coats of dope applied to eliminate dope _____ .

27. A _____ compound may be incorporated only in the first clear coat of dope to prevent loss in strength of fabric due to growth of _____ .

28. When re-covering or repairing control surface fabric, the repairs must not involve the addition of weight _____ or it will induce _____ .

29. A doped-on repair may be made on all aircraft fabric-covered surfaces provided the aircraft never-exceed speed is not greater than _____ .

30. A doped-on patch repair may be used if the damage does not exceed _____ in any direction.

Chapter 2
Fabric Covering

MULTIPLE CHOICE QUESTIONS

name:

date:

1. Which of these materials is the standard fabric covering for today's planes per the FAA?
   a. Polyester
   b. Linen
   c. Grade A cotton
   d. Silk

2. Which of these coverings is not actually approved for airplanes, but is part of an approved system of re-covering covered in a Supplemental Type Certificate?
   a. Polyester
   b. Linen
   c. Grade A cotton
   d. Silk

3. Which of these is a cut that is a continuous series of V's to prevent material from raveling?
   a. Bias
   b. Pinking
   c. Selvage
   d. Weft

4. Which process involves dipping the cotton fabric in a hot solution of diluted caustic soda to shrink and strengthen the material?
   a. Denier
   b. Sizing
   c. Calendering
   d. Mercerizing

5. If a fabric punch tester indicates that the aircraft fabric strength is marginal, what must be done?
   a. A laboratory test must be performed to determine actual fabric strength
   b. All of the fabric must be re-covered in accordance with an STC
   c. AC 43.13-1B states the fabric punch test is a sufficient testing device; no further action needed
   d. All of the fabric must be replaced in accordance with a TSO

6. Once the wing is covered, which of these is difficult to inspect thoroughly and even more difficult to repair and replace should they malfunction?
   a. Anti-drag wires
   b. Wing spars
   c. Aileron controls
   d. Bonding jumpers

7. The electrical conductivity of the aircraft structure will be impaired if which of the following becomes loose?
   a. Bonding jumpers
   b. Aileron controls
   c. Drag wires
   d. Vortex generators

8. Which of these is not a method for dope proofing the structure?
   a. Covering the structure with thin sheets of aluminum foil
   b. Covering the structure with padding
   c. Application of a layer of cellulose tape
   d. Applying a dope proof paint

9. To facilitate a high-quality, professional job of covering, which of these should be done?
   a. The structure should be thoroughly dope proofed
   b. All materials should be ordered in advance
   c. The fabric should have dope applied to it as soon as it is properly attached to the structure and shrunk
   d. The structure should be thoroughly inspected, repaired or replaced as necessary and placed in a holding fixture

Chapter 2
Fabric Covering

MULTIPLE CHOICE QUESTIONS

name:

date:

10. When ordering fabric for recovering, it is prudent to increase the order amount by how much to allow for mistakes, spoilage or waste?
    a. 3-5%
    b. 5-10%
    c. 10-20%
    d. 10-15%

11. Of the machine-sewn seams, which is the strongest?
    a. Modified folded fell seam sewn in two steps
    b. Plain overlap seam, straight edge
    c. Folded fell seam
    d. French fell seam

12. Which of these fabrics would not be a good choice for most re-coverings?
    a. 1.7-weight polyester
    b. 3.4-weight polyester
    c. 3.4-weight Mercerized cotton
    d. 1.7-weight linen

13. Which fabric is the strongest and most resistant to punctures and tears, and is therefore used most often on aircraft that are operated in rugged environments?
    a. 2.7-weight polyester
    b. 3.4-weight polyester
    c. 3.4-weight Mercerized cotton
    d. 1.7-weight linen

14. To pass an inspection, a fabric-covered airplane must maintain what percentage of the minimum tensile strength?
    a. 80
    b. 75
    c. 70
    d. 65

15. Which type of tape is used to stabilize the ribs before they are covered?
    a. Inter-rib bracing tape
    b. Anti-chafe tape
    c. Reinforcing tape
    d. Rib-reinforcing tape

16. Which type of tape is designed particularly for certain high-speed airplanes that need additional reinforcement to prevent the fabric covering from tearing?
    a. Fabric-reinforcing tape
    b. Bracing tape
    c. Anti-chafe tape
    d. Anti-tear tape

17. Which of these is necessary when the covering method requires the envelope method for covering the wing?
    a. Hand-sewing thread
    b. Machine-sewing thread
    c. Rib-stitching cord
    d. Linen thread

18. Which of these is needed to shield the fabric from the effects of ultraviolet rays?
    a. Two coats of color-pigmented dope
    b. Two coats of aluminum-pigmented dope
    c. Two coats of polyurethane finish
    d. Two coats of zinc dimethyldithiocarbamate

Chapter 2
Fabric Covering

MULTIPLE CHOICE QUESTIONS

name:

date:

19. Special ventilated masks should be worn when applying which of these, as they can be deadly?
    a. Aluminum-pigmented dope
    b. Zinc dimethyldithiocarbamate
    c. Polyurethane finish
    d. Butylnitrate dope

20. The envelope method of installation is not used with which of these materials?
    a. Irish linen
    b. Grade A cotton
    c. Aircraft linen
    d. Polyester fabric

21. Which of these materials is shrunk using heat?
    a. Irish linen
    b. Grade A cotton
    c. Aircraft linen
    d. Polyester fabric

22. Which of these is added to dope to slow down the rate of evaporation, allowing the dope to be brushed on the surface?
    a. Plasticizers
    b. Solvents
    c. Anti-blush compounds
    d. Dilutents

23. Which of these is added to dope to prevent or control whitening and retard drying of dope in a damp atmosphere?
    a. Plasticizers
    b. Solvents
    c. Anti-blush compounds
    d. Dilutents

24. Which of these are not allowed in the doping room under any circumstances?
    a. Air exchange by forced draft
    b. Electrical appliances
    c. Humidity of 45-55%
    d. Sprinkling water on the floor before sweeping

25. Under no circumstances will any airplane surface be finished with:
    a. More than three coats of dope if it is a light aircraft
    b. More than five coats of dope if higher wing-load aircraft
    c. Clear dope only
    d. Aluminum-pigmented colors

26. Which of these is caused by relative humidity being too high and can seriously reduce the tensile strength of dope film?
    a. Blushing
    b. Cellulose ester precipitation
    c. Acetic acid
    d. Dilution of the dope

27. Which of these is the only material that can be used if roughness appears on the surface after the final coats of dope?
    a. Pumice
    b. Steel wool
    c. Number 280 sandpaper
    d. Hog-bristle brush

Chapter 2
Fabric Covering

MULTIPLE CHOICE QUESTIONS

name:

date:

28. Which of these is not a necessary precaution when using dope?
    a. Do not use electrical equipment in the same area.
    b. Dope must be poured on fabric.
    c. Dope dispensing cans must be covered to prevent evaporation.
    d. Dope must not be exposed to air for more than an hour.

29. Which of these can be sprayed on a fabric surface to soften the coats of dope and help restore the condition of the coating?
    a. Rejuvenator
    b. Restorer
    c. Castor oil
    d. Butyric acid

30. Which of these repair methods on a fabric surface is preferred by many because a well-finished repair will all but disappear?
    a. Doped-in patch
    b. Sewn-in patch
    c. Doped-on panel
    d. Sewn-in panel

Chapter 2
Fabric Covering

ANALYSIS QUESTIONS

name:

date:

1. Describe some safety precautions you would observe when applying dope to a fabric-covered aircraft fuselage.

2. The owner of a vintage aircraft wants you to replace the aircraft's fabric covering. The aircraft has its original cotton fabric, which the owner wants to replace with polyester. How should you proceed?

3. An aircraft buyer has hired you to perform a pre-purchase inspection on a fabric covered aircraft with a metal tube fuselage and a wooden wing spar. The aircraft is parked in an old hangar with a dirt floor. The seller tells you the fabric punch tested fine on its last annual. How should you proceed?

4. In the example given above, what other factors should concern you?

5. Describe the relationship between thread count and tensile strength for cotton aircraft covering cloth.

6. What is the difference between reinforcing tape and surface tape?

7. What is the purpose of anti-tear tape, and when is it used?

8. Why do we perform pre-covering inspections?

9. What is the most important consideration when applying dope to fabric?

Chapter 2
Fabric Covering

ANALYSIS QUESTIONS

name:

date:

10. What do dope additives (fungicide and aluminum powder) have in common?

11. How does the sizing process differ between cotton fabric and polyester fabric?

12. What single factor has the most bearing on your decision to add plasticizers or antiblush compounds to the dope before applying it?

13. What factors determine the amount of dope (number of applications) that you apply when re-covering a wing?

14. What critical factor must you consider when performing a fabric repair on a control surface?

15. What determines if you can apply a doped-in patch repair?

Chapter 3
Materials and Processes

FILL IN THE BLANK QUESTIONS

name:

date:

1. The ability of a material to withstand forces that tend to deform it and to resist stress without breaking is known as _____.

2. A metal that can be hammered into various shapes without cracking or breaking is considered _____.

3. Metal that easily transmits heat or electricity has high _____.

4. Two to three tons of _____ are required to create one ton of alumina. Two tons of alumina are required to produce one ton of _____.

5. Producing recycled aluminum takes _____ % of the energy required to make new aluminum, and generates only _____ % as much greenhouse gas emissions.

6. A sheet of aluminum is between _____ and _____ inches thick. Any rolled piece of aluminum thicker than that is called a _____.

7. The _____ process involves aluminum (or another metal) being forced through a die with a shaped opening.

8. Aircraft engine crankcases are formed through _____ casting.

9. _____ is a process where metal is pressed, pounded, or squeezed into high-strength parts.

10. A standard Boeing 747 jumbo jet contains about _____ kilograms of aluminum.

11. A piece of aluminum weighs _____ as much as the same size piece of steel.

12. Aluminum, titanium, copper, and magnesium are called _____ because they have elements other than iron as their principal constituent.

13. _____ alloys are aluminum alloys that can be strengthened by heating and cooling.

14. Rivets made from _____ or _____ alloy must be heat treated before use.

15. _____ and _____ are nickel alloys.

16. Some aircraft parts commonly made of _____ include exhaust collectors, stacks, manifolds, structural and machined parts, springs, castings, tie rods, and control cables.

Chapter 3
Materials and Processes

FILL IN THE BLANK QUESTIONS

name:

date:

17. In general, _____ is the opposite of hardening.

18. The process of _____ steel removes internal stresses set up by welding, machining, forming, or other types of handling.

19. Brinell, Rockwell, Vickers, and Webster are methods of _____ testing.

20. _____ fasteners comprise two parts—a pin and a collar with a fracture section that shears off at a predetermined torque.

21. The unthreaded portion of a standard or flush-head pin is called the _____ .

22. The recommended speed for drilling aluminum alloy is _____ to _____ surface feet per minute (SFM). For mild steel, the recommended speed is _____ to _____ SFM.

23. To drill a hole in hard material, use _____ speed and _____ pressure.

24. When deep drilling aluminum, titanium, or corrosion-resistant steel, a _____-based lubricant is recommended.

25. _____ is used to create a cone-shaped well at the end of a hole to accommodate a fastener head or rivet head.

26. Rivet countersinks in areas exposed to the airstream should be cut so the finished head is _____ inches higher than the surface of the skin on small holes, and _____ inches higher on larger holes.

27. A sheet holder, commonly called a _____ , holds parts tightly in place in order to maintain hole alignment during drilling and fastener installation.

28. _____ is the preferred method for making a large hole in metal.

29. An installed _____ includes two heads—the manufactured head and the _____ head (or bucktail) formed at the time of driving.

30. A rivet made of 2117 aluminum goes by the alloy code _____ . Its head is marked with a _____ .

31. Rivet size and diameter are indicated in _____ of an inch. Thus, a rivet size of 6-8 indicates a diameter of _____ of an inch and a length of _____ of an inch.

Chapter 3
Materials and Processes

FILL IN THE BLANK QUESTIONS

name:

date:

32. _____ rivets have a mushroom shape, a head diameter twice the shank diameter, and a head height approximately 42.5% of the shank diameter.

33. In team riveting, one tap means _____ . Three taps means _____ .

34. When sheet metal is _____ , the angle formed will follow the arc of a circle.

35. The term _____ refers to the flat distance of the section of metal that will be curved in bending.

36. The lines that mark the boundaries of a bend to be made, or where the bent metal will meet the unbent metal, are called _____ .

37. The _____ is the standard piece of equipment for bending large sheets of metal.

38. When forming sheet metal into a box shape, _____ must be cut in the corners to prevent an intense concentration of stress.

39. Bumping, forming, and crimping are types of _____ operations used to shape metal.

40. An English wheel is a forming tool that can be used to create _____ in sheet metal.

Chapter 3
Materials and Processes

MULTIPLE CHOICE QUESTIONS

name:

date:

1. Which of the following is **NOT** a property of metal?
   a. Strength
   b. Conductivity
   c. Elasticity
   d. Productivity

2. Which term refers to the property of metal that allows it to be permanently drawn, bent, or twisted into various shapes without breaking?
   a. Hardness
   b. Density
   c. Ductility
   d. Brittleness

3. Which term refers to the property of metal that allows it to return to its original shape when the force that caused the change of shape is removed?
   a. Elasticity
   b. Hardness
   c. Density
   d. Ductility

4. Rolled aluminum that is less than 0.0079 inches thick is called:
   a. Foil
   b. Alumina
   c. Plate
   d. Sheet

5. Pouring molten metal into a form is part of the process known as:
   a. Forging
   b. Casting
   c. Extrusion
   d. Cold rolling

6. Pounding, pressing, or squeezing aluminum under pressure into a high-strength part is called:
   a. Forging
   b. Casting
   c. Extrusion
   d. Cold rolling

7. A piece of aluminum in an alloy identification number that starts with 7 is alloyed with which of these metals?
   a. Copper
   b. Manganese
   c. Iron
   d. Zinc

8. Which of these is the lightest structural metal in the world and weighs two-thirds as much as aluminum, with which it is often alloyed?
   a. Nickel
   b. Magnesium
   c. Titanium
   d. Tin

9. Which of these is **NOT** a ferrous metal?
   a. Iron
   b. Steel
   c. Aluminum
   d. Carbon steel

10. If you heat steel to just above the critical temperature, soak it at that temperature, and cool it slowly in a furnace, this process is called:
    a. Annealing
    b. Normalizing
    c. Tempering
    d. None of these

Chapter 3
Materials and Processes

MULTIPLE CHOICE QUESTIONS

name:

date:

11. A process that reduces brittleness and softens steel, involving heating the steel to more than 212° F and cooling it in still air, is called:
    a. Annealing
    b. Normalizing
    c. Tempering
    d. None of these

12. Steel parts that require a hard, wear-resistant surface can be:
    a. Carburized
    b. Annealed
    c. Tempered
    d. Hardness tested

13. Which hardness testing system scales the hardness of a metal based on the depth of penetration of a diamond cone or steel ball under major and minor loads?
    a. Brinnell
    b. Rockwell
    c. Vickers
    d. Webster

14. A fastener with the strength of a bolt, quick assembly time, and a pin/collar assembly with some degree of disassembly allowed is called a:
    a. Hi-Lok fastener
    b. Rivet
    c. Sheer pin
    d. Lockbolt

15. Permanent fastener assemblies that use a headed pin with a collar that are used primarily in heavy structures requiring high shear and clamp-up values are called:
    a. Hi-Lok fasteners
    b. Rivets
    c. Sheer pins
    d. Lockbolts

16. At what r.p.m. should a ¼-inch drill turn to drill aluminum at 250 SFM?
    a. 3,500 r.p.m.
    b. 3,800 r.p.m.
    c. 4,000 r.p.m.
    d. 4,200 r.p.m.

17. Which of these general rules for drilling is wrong?
    a. Big drill, low speed, high pressure
    b. Hard material, lower speed, higher pressure
    c. Small drill, high speed, light pressure
    d. Big drill, hard material, high speed

18. Drill diameters are classified by three size standards. Which of these is not one of them?
    a. Length
    b. Number
    c. Letter
    d. Fractional

19. Which countersink works best in aluminum?
    a. Four-fluted
    b. Twelve-fluted
    c. Single-flute Weldon type
    d. Six-fluted

20. What drill accessory is used to enlarge holes or finish them smoothly to the required size?
    a. Reamer
    b. Countersink
    c. Bushing
    d. Cleco

Chapter 3
Materials and Processes

MULTIPLE CHOICE QUESTIONS

name:

date:

21. What fastener fits this definition: "a pin of malleable material that becomes a fastener when the ends are upset to form heads."
    a. Hi-Lok
    b. Rivet
    c. Lockbolt
    d. Rivnut

22. Which of these are examples of universal-head rivets?
    a. MS20615 and BACR15BB
    b. BACR15FT and MS20470
    c. MS20426 and BACR15BA
    d. NAS1097 and BACR15CE

23. Which of these are examples of standard flush-head rivets?
    a. MS20615 and BACR15BB
    b. BACR15FT and MS20470
    c. MS20426 and BACR15BA
    d. NAS1097 and BACR15CE

24. The standard practice in installing a protruding-head rivet is to place the factory head against the:
    a. Thicker sheet of metal
    b. Outside of the aircraft
    c. Inside the aircraft
    d. Thinner sheet of metal

25. Which rivet installation process makes an indentation around a rivet hole but removes no metal?
    a. NACA
    b. Countersinking
    c. Dimpling
    d. Protruding-head method

26. The preferred circumference of the installed formed head of a D, E, KE, or M rivet is:
    a. 1.25 times the circumference of the shank
    b. 1.5 times the circumference of the shank
    c. 1.66 times the circumference of the shank
    d. 0.5 times the circumference of the shank

27. An installed rivet, upon inspection, has a crack about 1/10 as wide as the rivet shank diameter. What should you do?
    a. Consult FAA manuals for the rivet type in question.
    b. Leave the rivet in place; it is satisfactory.
    c. Call the rivet manufacturer's help desk.
    d. Remove the rivet and replace it.

28. The formed head of an installed rivet is off-center, but not enough for the hole to be visible beside it. What should you do?
    a. Consult FAA manuals for the rivet type in question.
    b. Leave the rivet in place; it is satisfactory.
    c. Call the rivet manufacturer's help desk.
    d. Remove the rivet and replace it.

29. A line from the edge of a piece of metal to the point in space where lines extended from the outside surfaces of either side of a bend is called what?
    a. Inside dimension
    b. Neutral line
    c. Bend tangent line
    d. Mold-line dimension

30. The width of a piece of sheet metal, from one edge around a bend to the other edge is called:
    a. Total developed width
    b. Bend allowance
    c. Bend radius
    d. Material growth

Chapter 3
Materials and Processes

MULTIPLE CHOICE QUESTIONS

name:

date:

31. Calculate the bend allowance (the length of material required) for a 90° bend. The metal is 0.44 inches thick and the radius of the bend is 0.5 inches.
    a. 4.65 inches
    b. 1.16 inches
    c. 2.32 inches
    d. 3 inches

32. Calculate the setback for the bend in Question 31:
    a. 90.44 inches
    b. 0.94 inches
    c. 0.74 inches
    d. 1.16 inches

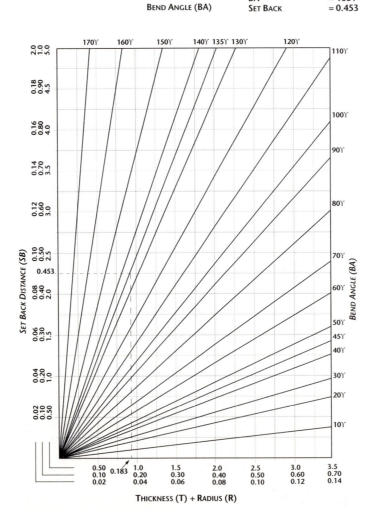

Figure 1.

33. Using the chart in Figure 1, determine the setback distance for a 120° bend in a piece of metal that is 0.6 inches thick. The bend radius is 0.4 inches.
    a. About 1.72 inches
    b. About 1.52 inches
    c. About 1.78 inches
    d. About 0.183 inches

34. Using the chart in Figure 1, determine the setback distance for an 80° bend in a piece of metal that is 0.2 inches thick. The bend radius is 0.3 inches.
    a. About 0.53 inches
    b. About 0.43 inches
    c. About 0.453 inches
    d. About 0.083 inches

35. Using the K chart in Figure 2, determine the K-value for a 112° bend.
    a. 0.78128
    b. 0.80879
    c. 0.4826
    d. 1.4826

Chapter 3
Materials and Processes

MULTIPLE CHOICE QUESTIONS

name:

date:

SETBACK CHART (K CHART)							
1°	0.00873	37°	0.33459	73°	0.73996	109°	1.4019	145°	3.1716
2°	0.01745	38°	0.34433	74°	0.75355	110°	1.4281	146°	3.2708
3°	0.02618	39°	0.35412	75°	0.76733	111°	1.4550	147°	3.3759
4°	0.03492	40°	0.36397	76°	0.78128	112°	1.4826	148°	3.4874
5°	0.04366	41°	0.37388	77°	0.79546	113°	1.5108	149°	3.6059
6°	0.05241	42°	0.38386	78°	0.80978	114°	1.5399	150°	3.7320
7°	0.06116	43°	0.39391	79°	0.82434	115°	1.5697	151°	3.8667
8°	0.06993	44°	0.40403	80°	0.83910	116°	1.6003	152°	4.0108
9°	0.07870	45°	0.41421	81°	0.85408	117°	1.6318	153°	4.1653
10°	0.08749	46°	0.42447	82°	0.86929	118°	1.6643	154°	4.3315
11°	0.09629	47°	0.43481	83°	0.88472	119°	1.6977	155°	4.5107
12°	0.10510	48°	0.44523	84°	0.90040	120°	1.7320	156°	4.7046
13°	0.11393	49°	0.45573	85°	0.91633	121°	1.7675	157°	4.9151
14°	0.12278	50°	0.46631	86°	0.93251	122°	1.8040	158°	5.1455
15°	0.13165	51°	0.47697	87°	0.94896	123°	1.8418	159°	5.3995
16°	0.14054	52°	0.48773	88°	0.96569	124°	1.8807	160°	5.6713
17°	0.14945	53°	0.49858	89°	0.98270	125°	1.9210	161°	5.9758
18°	0.15838	54°	0.50952	90°	1.00000	126°	1.9626	162°	6.3137
19°	0.16734	55°	0.52057	91°	1.0176	127°	2.0057	163°	6.6911
20°	0.17633	56°	0.53171	92°	1.0355	128°	2.0503	164°	7.1154
21°	0.18534	57°	0.54295	93°	1.0538	129°	2.0965	165°	7.5957
22°	0.19438	58°	0.55431	94°	1.0724	130°	2.1445	166°	8.1443
23°	0.20345	59°	0.56577	95°	1.0913	131°	2.1943	167°	8.7769
24°	0.21256	60°	0.57735	96°	1.1106	132°	2.2460	168°	9.5144
25°	0.22169	61°	0.58904	97°	1.1303	133°	2.2998	169°	10.385
26°	0.23087	62°	0.60086	98°	1.1504	134°	2.3558	170°	11.430
27°	0.24008	63°	0.61280	99°	1.1708	135°	2.4142	171°	12.706
28°	0.24933	64°	0.62487	100°	1.1917	136°	2.4751	172°	14.301
29°	0.25862	65°	0.63707	101°	1.2131	137°	2.5386	173°	16.350
30°	0.26795	66°	0.64941	102°	1.2349	138°	2.6051	174°	19.081
31°	0.27732	67°	0.66188	103°	1.2572	139°	2.6746	175°	22.904
32°	0.28674	68°	0.67451	104°	1.2799	140°	2.7475	176°	26.636
33°	0.29621	69°	0.68728	105°	1.3032	141°	2.8239	177°	38.188
34°	0.30573	70°	0.70021	106°	1.3270	142°	2.9042	178°	57.290
35°	0.31530	71°	0.71329	107°	1.3514	143°	2.9887	179°	114.590
36°	0.32492	72°	0.72654	108°	1.3764	144°	3.0777	180°	Infinite

Figure 2.

Chapter 3
Materials and Processes

MULTIPLE CHOICE QUESTIONS

name:

date:

36. Calculate the setback distance for a 25° bend in a piece of metal that is 0.35 inches thick. The bend radius is 3/8 of an inch.
    a. 1 inch
    b. 0.161 inches
    c. 0.222 inches
    d. 0.611 inches

37. Which of these sheet metal brakes is sometimes called a finger brake?
    a. Cornice brake
    b. Box and pan brake
    c. Press brake
    d. Bar folder

38. What is best suited to bending small hems, flanges, seams, or edges in sheet metal?
    a. Cornice brake
    b. Box and pan brake
    c. Press brake
    d. Bar folder

39. Hammering a piece of metal so that the material becomes thinner in one area and the piece bends is called:
    a. Bumping
    b. Crimping
    c. Stretching
    d. Shrinking

40. Hammering metal into a new shape while it is on a die or sandbag is called:
    a. Bumping
    b. Crimping
    c. Stretching
    d. Shrinking

Chapter 3
Materials and Processes

ANALYSIS QUESTIONS

name:

date:

1. Describe briefly the process by which a sheet of aluminum is manufactured, beginning with the collection of the raw materials.

2. Describe the value of aluminum recycling.

3. What are the advantages of forged aluminum over cast aluminum?

4. Describe the aluminum alloy numbering system. What does an alloy identifier that starts with 6 indicate?

5. What are the types of annealing used with aluminum alloys, and what is the goal of each?

6. When replacing metal on an aircraft, what are four factors you should take into consideration?

7. What is the best method for determining the temperature of steel? What method is the least accurate?

Chapter 3
Materials and Processes

ANALYSIS
QUESTIONS

name:

date:

8. What are the advantages of Hi-Lok fasteners over rivets? What are the advantages of rivets?

9. Describe how you can start a drill hole in a precise location.

10. What are some safety precautions to take when installing rivets?

11. Calculate the bend allowance for a 100° bend in material 0.045 inches thick. The bend radius is 3/8 of an inch. Give your answer to the nearest thousandth of an inch.

12. Calculate the setback for the bend described in Question 11.

13. Calculate the material growth in the bend described in Question 11.

14. Use the J chart in Figure 3 to figure the developed length of a piece of metal. The mold line dimensions are 2 inches on one side of the bend and 3 inches on the other side. The material is 0.070 inches thick, the bend radius is ¼ inch, and the angle of the bend is 70°.

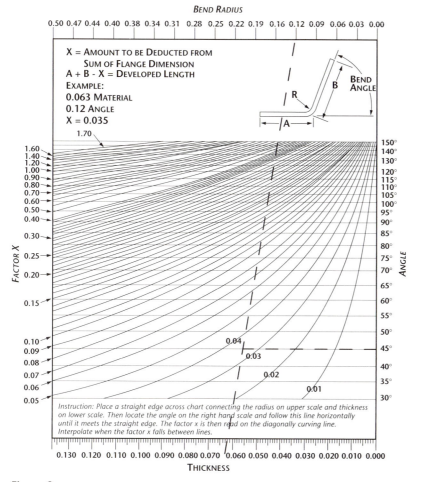

Figure 3.

15. Briefly describe the five main methods of hand-forming metal.

Chapter 3
Materials and Processes

ANALYSIS QUESTIONS

name:

date:

Chapter 4
Airframe Metallic Structures

FILL IN THE BLANK QUESTIONS

name:

date:

1. The basic type of _____ construction in modern helicopters and airplanes is monocoque.

2. In a monocoque construction, the _____ carries the major stresses and functions as part of the airframe.

3. On most multi-engine airplanes, the power plants are housed in _____ .

4. Generally, the metals used in fuselage construction are _____ alloys known commercially as 7075-T and 2024-T.

5. In general, wing construction is based on one of three fundamental designs: mono-spar, _____ , or _____ .

6. The section of the aircraft that includes the aft end of the fuselage or the booms, rudders, stabilizers, elevators, and trim tabs is called the _____ .

7. The main lengthwise members of an airframe structure are _____ and _____.

8. _____ is most likely to occur in pockets and corners where moisture, dirt and salt spray accumulate.

9. The most severe damage to an airframe is classified as _____ .

10. During repairs to the airframe, the aircraft must be adequately _____ to prevent further distortion or damage.

11. If the _____ in repair skin metal do not exactly match those in the aircraft structure, additional stress will be placed on the rivets.

12. To repair a circular hole in metal aircraft skin, you can make a _____ if the hole does not exceed 1-3/4 inch diameter.

13. A damaged stringer may be patched if the damage does not exceed _____ of the width of one leg and is less than _____ inches long.

14. It may not be possible to repair a spar because of the critical stresses imposed on them, but if a repair is made, it is usually accomplished by _____ .

15. _____ is a temporary repair performed to relieve the concentrated stress causing a crack. Use a _____ inch hole at each end and at each sharp turn of the crack.

Chapter 4
Airframe Metallic Structures

FILL IN THE BLANK QUESTIONS

name:

date:

16. _____ is the distance from the edge of the material being fastened to the centerline of the fastener hole. Another term for it is _____ .

17. When patching 0.025-inch-thick corrosion-resistant steel, you should use a patch that is _____ inches thick made out of _____ .

18. The strength of fasteners should be such that their total shear strength is approximately equal to the _____ of the material.

19. Stress on a joint is calculated as the _____ divided by the _____ . It is measured, most often, in pounds per _____ .

20. The formula for rivet shear is the same as the basic formula for joint stress except that it includes the _____ of the rivets.

21. A scratch or gouge on sheet metal reduces the _____ of the sheet and it therefore considered a _____ .

22. To calculate the maximum load that a joint can withstand, multiply the _____ by the _____ .

23. A joint can fail in four ways: _____ , _____ , _____ , or _____ .

24. If a certain material gauge is not available for repairing a back-up structure, use the _____ gauge.

25. If an angle in a structural assembly is damaged, but the damage is confined to one flange and doesn't penetrate the radius, it is considered a _____ damage.

Chapter 4
Airframe Metallic Structures

MULTIPLE CHOICE QUESTIONS

name:

date:

1. What two modifications of the full monocoque fuselage were developed to increase load-carrying capacity?
   a. Semi-monocoque and quasi-monocoque
   b. Bulkhead and former
   c. Reinforced shell and semi-monocoque
   d. Reinforced shell and semi-reinforced shell

2. Name the main structural unit of an airplane:
   a. Longeron
   b. Fuselage
   c. Cabin section
   d. Nacelle

3. Which of these is the primary concern in the design of engine mounts?
   a. To make the engine and its equipment accessible for maintenance and inspection
   b. To make the engines function more efficiently
   c. To hold the engine fast to the fuselage
   d. To make the engine impervious to vibration

4. Which of the following statements regarding turbine engine mounts is not true?
   a. They are subjected to high-vibration inertial loads.
   b. They operate in high-temperature environments.
   c. They are susceptible to improper torque fittings.
   d. They are susceptible to fatigue failure from their loading environment.

5. What are the principle structural members of an aircraft wing?
   a. Box beams
   b. Ribs
   c. Nacelles
   d. Spars

6. In an I-beam spar, what are the two cap strips connected by?
   a. Stringer
   b. Web
   c. Hat section
   d. Rivets

7. Which of these items provides the major cross-sectional support for a fuselage?
   a. Bulkhead
   b. Frame
   c. Former
   d. Gusset

8. What are the heavy lengthwise members of an aircraft structure called?
   a. Frames
   b. Gussets
   c. Longerons
   d. Stringers

9. What are the two most common cross-section shapes of stringers?
   a. J shaped
   b. Z shaped
   c. T shaped
   d. Hat section

10. What is the term for a rivet that has movement under structural stress, but which has not loosened to the extent that movement can be observed?
    a. Walking rivet
    b. Corroded rivet
    c. Head rivet
    d. Working rivet

Chapter 4
Airframe Metallic Structures

MULTIPLE CHOICE QUESTIONS

name:

date:

11. Damage that does not affect the structural integrity of the member involved, or that can be corrected simply without placing flight restrictions on the aircraft is called what?
    a. Negligible damage
    b. Damage repairable by patching
    c. Transient damage
    d. Damage repairable by insertion

12. What type of structural member varies in thickness from one end to the other or from one side to the other?
    a. Aluminum alloy
    b. Chrome-molybdenum steel tubing
    c. Alclad aluminum
    d. Chem-milled

13. If the edges of the patch and the aircraft skin overlap, the patch is called:
    a. A lap or scab patch
    b. A flush or lap patch
    c. A flush or scab patch
    d. An open-skin patch

14. If the skin of an aircraft is accessible from both sides, it is called:
    a. Open skin
    b. Closed skin
    c. Outside skin
    d. Interior skin

15. Why should you drill small holes at each end of a crack or small hole before applying a patch?
    a. To insert rivets
    b. It relieves stress and keeps the crack from spreading
    c. To clean the metal and provide a better bond for the patch
    d. To enhance airflow around that portion of the skin

16. Which of these methods for marking a new metal panel is NOT acceptable?
    a. Aircraft marking pencil
    b. Transfer punch
    c. Number 2 pencil
    d. Hole finder

17. Two methods of repairing ribs and longerons are:
    a. Patching and visual inspection
    b. Patching and reinforcement
    c. Patching and insertion
    d. Patching and spar web repair

18. How many fasteners would be required if a repair specification calls for 12 equal spaces between fasteners?
    a. 12
    b. 10
    c. 11
    d. 13

19. What is the minimum distance from an edge that a rivet with a diameter of 3/16 inch can be placed?
    a. 7/16 inch
    b. 5/16 inch
    c. 3/32 inch
    d. 3/16 inch

20. What type of seal is usually installed at points where frequent breaking of the seal is necessary (like on an entrance door)?
    a. Special seal
    b. Sealing compound
    c. Rubber seal
    d. Retainer seal

21. What type of seal is usually installed at places where the seal will only be broken for structural repairs or part replacement?
    a. Special seal
    b. Sealing compound
    c. Rubber seal
    d. Retainer seal

22. In a riveted joint, if a sheet separates or breaks, it is called:
    a. Rivet shear failure
    b. Tear-out failure
    c. Tensile failure
    d. Bearing failure

23. In a riveted joint, if holes in a sheet get longer, it is called:
    a. Rivet shear failure
    b. Tear-out failure
    c. Tensile failure
    d. Bearing failure

24. The cross-sectional area of a sheet including the holes is called the:
    a. Gross area
    b. Net area
    c. Tensile area
    d. Thickness

25. If two sheets of metal are joined by rivets and the holes in the sheet elongate, this is called:
    a. Tear-out failure
    b. Bearing failure
    c. Rivet shear failure
    d. Tensile failure

26. If two sheets of metal are joined by rivets and the sheets tear, this is called:
    a. Tear-out failure
    b. Bearing failure
    c. Rivet shear failure
    d. Tensile failure

27. If two sheets of metal are joined by rivets and rivets break, this is called:
    a. Tear-out failure
    b. Bearing failure
    c. Rivet shear failure
    d. Tensile failure

28. If two sheets of metal are joined by rivets and the sheets separate or break, this is called:
    a. Tear-out failure
    b. Bearing failure
    c. Rivet shear failure
    d. Tensile failure

Chapter 4
Airframe Metallic Structures

MULTIPLE CHOICE QUESTIONS

name:

date:

Chapter 4
Airframe Metallic Structures

MULTIPLE CHOICE QUESTIONS

name:

date:

29. Force is calculated by dividing the pressure by the area. What is another way to express this formula?
    a. Power=Load/Stress
    b. Stress=Load/Area
    c. Stress=Pounds/Square Inch
    d. Both B and C

30. The basic formula for calculating maximum load is:
    a. F=P x A
    b. P=S x A
    c. P=F x A
    d. F=A/P

31. A joint will fail in the failure mode with the:
    a. Lowest maximum force
    b. Lowest maximum load
    c. Greatest tensile stress
    d. Most manageable rivet shear stress

32. What document lists the type of materials used in an aircraft structure?
    a. Manufacturer's Airframe Handbook
    b. Manufacturer's Material Identification Guide
    c. Manufacturer's Maintenance Manual
    d. Manufacturer's Structural Repair Manual

33. According to Table 4-4-1 (on page 4-48), what rivet diameter should be used on 0.045 gauge material?
    a. 3/32 inch
    b. 1/8 inch
    c. 5/32 inch
    d. 3/16 inch

34. Besides being used to repair skin punctures, a circular repair is also often used:
    a. Where an access hole had to be cut
    b. Over a lightening hole
    c. Where a crack of any length forms
    d. On ribs or formers

Chapter 4
Airframe Metallic Structures

ANALYSIS QUESTIONS

name:

date:

1. Describe the three main types of wing construction. On what types of aircraft is each one used?

2. What are the three principles that apply to almost all structural repairs? What are some ways in which each one is put into practice?

3. Describe how damage to aircraft structural parts is classified.

4. Describe the process for replacing a small portion of an aircraft's metal skin.

5. A repair specification calls for 10 equal spaces between fasteners. Assume that the distance between the first and last fastener will be 12 inches. Describe how you would calculate the distance between fasteners.

6. Two sheets of aluminum alloy are riveted together with three rivets. The sheets are 4 inches wide and 0.040 inches thick. The holes for the 0.125-inch-diameter rivets are drilled at 0.1285 inches in diameter. The edge distance (ED) is 2d. A load of 800 pounds is applied to the joint. What is the tension stress on this joint?

Chapter 4
Airframe Metallic Structures

ANALYSIS QUESTIONS

name:

date:

7. Using the situation in Question 6, calculate the rivet shear stress.

8. Using the situation in Question 6, calculate the bearing stress.

9. Using the situation in Question 6, calculate the tear-out stress.

10. Two sheets of 2024-T3 clad are joined by four rivets. The sheets are 5 inches wide and 0.063 inches thick. The holes for the 0.09-inch-diameter rivets are drilled at 0.1 inches in diameter. The edge distance (ED) is 2d. Use 35,000 as the F_{su} when calculating rivet shear. Look up the other ultimate strength numbers in Table 6-3-1 using basis A in the column for the given thickness and row LT. What are the maximum tensile, rivet shear, bearing, and tear-out loads if the joint is tested to failure. In what mode with the joint fail first?

11. What are some of the safety precautions you should take when working with sheet metal?

Chapter 5
Airframe Nonmetallic Structures

FILL IN THE BLANK QUESTIONS

name:

date:

1. The combination of high **Strength to weight** ratios and automated manufacturing processes makes advanced composites a popular structural design component for modern aircraft.

2. The warp is the threads that run from one end of a roll of fabric to another. The **Bias** runs from side to side, at 90° to the warp.

3. **Resin** gives fiberglass form, and also carries loads from one fiber to the next.

4. Before inspecting the damage to reinforced plastic, the area should be cleaned with a cloth saturated in **MEK**. It should then be **sanded** lightly, and cleaned again.

5. Some types of damage to reinforced plastic can be filled with a mixture of resin and short-chopped cotton or fiberglass fibers called **Flox**.

6. To prevent corrosion inside a repaired metal honeycomb structure, the repair must be primed with a **corrosion inhibiting primer** that will completely seal the repaired area.

7. **advanced composites**, high-strength stiff fibers embedded in a matrix material, are being used to replace some of the metals currently used in aircraft construction.

8. Advanced composites are highly susceptible to **impact damage**, with the extent of damage being visually difficult to determine.

9. **Boron**, first developed in 1959, are one of the earliest advanced composite materials.

10. **Kevlar** cannot be cut with regular shears and must be drilled with a **brad-point drill** made for Arimid fabric.

11. A technician can control the bonding and curing process in an advanced composite repair using **Hot Bonding**.

12. A method for curing a composite repair that involves release films, bleeder and breather materials, and a heat blanket, among other things, is known as **vacuum bagging materials**.

13. A **laminate** is a stacked arrangement of lamina, also known as **plies**.

14. It is expected that new airframes will be **75-80** percent composites.

Chapter 5
Airframe Nonmetallic Structures

FILL IN THE BLANK QUESTIONS

name:

date:

15. When conducting a visual inspection of a composite structure, if you even suspect underlying damage, remove the __paint or protective coating__ from the area and shine a strong light through the structure to illuminate possible damage.

16. X-rays and __ultrasonic__ inspections are high-tech methods of assessing the damage to composite materials.

17. The SRM will often specify an aerodynamic __smoothness__ requirement for critical zones including the leading edges of wings and tails, forward nacelles and inlet areas, forward fuselages, and over-wing areas of the fuselage.

18. A __respirator__ equipped with a HEPA filter is required to protect against the dust generated in many advanced composite repair processes.

19. __Lexan__, like Plexiglas, are lighter than glass and easier to fabricate and repair.

20. More general aviation windows and windshields are ruined by __improper cleaning__ than by most other reasons combined.

21. Plexiglas can be bent along a straight line by using a __strip heater__ to make the material pliable.

22. To fasten high-strength joints between structural parts made of Plexiglas, use a __screwdriver__.

23. The first airplanes were not made of metal or composites, but of __wood__ or bamboo.

24. One popular training airplane with all-wood wings and center section is the __Stearman__, first built in 1941.

25. In repairs involving wooden parts, use a __plastic resin glue (urea-formaldehyde)__ adhesive rather than Casin glue.

Chapter 5
Airframe Nonmetallic Structures

MULTIPLE CHOICE QUESTIONS

name: _____

date: _____

1. Which of these statements about composite fuselage construction is true?
   a. Monocoque structures are more common in composite designs
   b. Composite structures simplify repairs, but make manufacturing more complex
   c. Composite wing designs are never used because of the stresses involved
   d. Nonmetallic materials cannot be used to create reinforced-shell constructions structures

2. Which type of fiberglass is used when higher chemical resistance is necessary?
   a. E glass
   b. S glass
   c. C glass
   d. I glass

3. When the woof in a fabric turns around at the edge of the cloth and goes back to the other side, it produces:
   a. A nacelle
   b. Bias
   c. A selvage
   d. Warp

4. Which of these statements about fiberglass is *not* true?
   a. It is composed of glass fibers spun into yarn, then woven
   b. The fabric is encased in a resin matrix
   c. Its strength is no match for that of aluminum
   d. Several layers of material are laminated together in a mold to form a part

5. Epoxy resin must be used within the time defined by its:
   a. Storage
   b. Pot life
   c. Half life
   d. Real life

6. What tool should be used to cut out the walls around ply damage to a solid laminate in preparation for a stepped repair?
   a. A chisel
   b. A router
   c. An X-acto knife
   d. A drill

7. Small repairs to honeycomb core and facing are best accomplished with which of these methods?
   a. Scarfed method
   b. Stepped method
   c. Complete part replacement
   d. Refinishing

8. When the fibers in a composite material are oriented in such a way that the part has the same strength in different directions, the composite is considered:
   a. Isotropic
   b. Quasi-isotropic
   c. Unidirectional
   d. Anisotropic

9. Which of these is not an advantage of composite parts over metal parts?
   a. Higher specific strengths
   b. Reduced production costs
   c. Excellent corrosion resistance
   d. Ease of inspection

10. The high-strength fibers produced by graphitizing filaments of rayon are known as:
    a. Carbon fibers
    b. Boron fibers
    c. Isotropic fibers
    d. Kevlar

Chapter 5
Airframe Nonmetallic Structures

MULTIPLE CHOICE QUESTIONS

name:

date:

11. A homogeneous resin that, when cured, forms the binder that holds the fibers together and transfers the load to the fibers in a composite is called:
    a. The glue
    b. The integrator
    c. The matrix (5-20)
    d. The lamina

12. Which of these statements about heat blankets is not true?
    a. The heat blanket transfers heat to the part via conduction
    b. Since heat rises, the heat blanket must be in contact only with the lower half of the part
    c. A heat blanket's wires and connectors should be inspected before use
    d. A heat blanket should overlap the area of the repair by a minimum of 2 inches on all sides

13. For areas larger than 2 square feet, which of these is incapable of providing more than 150°F (66°C)?
    a. Heat blanket
    b. Heat gun
    c. Hot air unit
    d. Heat lamp

14. Correct fiber contact during curing is induced by:
    a. Vacuum pressure
    b. Excess resin
    c. Heat blankets
    d. Ancillary materials

15. What is typically placed on top of a release film next to a curing part in order to allow removal of excess resins, air and volatile gases?
    a. Breather material
    b. Heat blanket
    c. Bleeder material
    d. A separator

16. In the stacking sequence [+90/+45/0/-45/-90], the fourth lamina is oriented:
    a. 45° right of the x-axis of the part
    b. 45° left of the x-axis of the part
    c. at a right angle to the x-axis of the part
    d. 45° left of the y-axis of the part

17. Damage such as crazing and cracking caused by solar and ultraviolet radiation, water absorbed through humidity and rain, and lightning-strike damage is classified as:
    a. Environmental damage
    b. Physical damage
    c. Laminate damage
    d. Catastrophic damage

18. What simple procedure can be used to locate delaminations, disbanding, core damage, or other damage close to the surface of composite materials?
    a. X-ray inspection
    b. Visual inspection
    c. Ultrasonic inspection
    d. Tap testing

19. Damage that is deeper than 0.015 inches, but that does not fully penetrate the aircraft skin or damage the honeycomb core is considered repairable damage of which type?
    a. Class II
    b. Class III
    c. Class IV
    d. Class V

Chapter 5
Airframe Nonmetallic Structures

MULTIPLE CHOICE QUESTIONS

name: _Jared Bird_

date:

20. Repair manuals should be consulted to ascertain the borders of these areas, as load-carrying requirements, skin thickness, ply drop-offs, location of supporting members, type of materials and other specifications can vary from one to the next.
    a. Repair zones
    b. Flaps
    c. **No-fly zones**
    d. Structural criteria

21. This composite repair tool should be operated at 25,000–40,000 r.p.m.
    a. Drill
    b. **Circular saw**
    c. Disk sander
    d. Router

22. Which of these should not be used to remove paint from composite surfaces?
    a. Jitterbug sander
    b. Media blasting
    c. Disk sander
    d. **DA sander**

23. How should epoxy resins should be disposed of?
    a. **They should be incinerated**
    b. Thrown away in liquid form in a sealed container
    c. Recycle them
    d. Let them cure and then throw them away

24. What is the most common and distracting type of damage found in aircraft transparencies?
    a. **Chemical damage**
    b. Crazing
    c. Paint overspray
    d. Yellowing

25. Which of these is not an advantage of Plexiglas over glass?
    a. Light weight
    b. **Ease of forming**
    c. Scratch resistance
    d. Easy to cut

26. To remove minor scratches from composite windows start sanding with:
    a. 220-grit dry sandpaper
    b. 1500 Micro-Mesh
    c. 4000 Micro-Mesh
    d. **2400 Micro-Mesh**

27. Plexiglas is resistant to which of these chemicals?
    a. **Carbon tetrachloride**
    b. Sulfuric acid
    c. Benzene
    d. Acetic acid

28. If the temperate increases 4°F, how much will a 10-inch-wide sheet of Plexiglas expand in width?
    a. 0.2 inches
    b. 0.0002 inches
    c. **0.00005 inches**
    d. 0.002 inches

Chapter 5
Airframe Nonmetallic Structures

MULTIPLE CHOICE QUESTIONS

name:

date:

29. Critical load-bearing Plexiglas joints should be cemented with:
    a. Plexiglas II cement
    b. Acrifix 116
    c. PS-18 cement
    d. 1-1-2 trichloroethylene

30. Which of the following is a softwood?
    a. Oak
    b. Mahogany
    c. Noble fir
    d. Birch

Chapter 5
Airframe Nonmetallic Structures

ANALYSIS QUESTIONS

name:

date:

1. Describe the process for repairing damage that affects more than one ply in a sandwich-type laminate.

2. Describe the process for repairing a damaged facing over a honeycomb core. Assume that the core is also damaged, but that the damage does not extend all the way through the part.

3. Define "advanced composite materials." What advanced composite materials are commonly used on aircraft? What advantages do they have over metals? What disadvantages?

4. Heat blankets are used to apply heat to composite repairs. What are some things you should keep in mind while using a heat blanket?

5. Vacuum bagging requires a number of materials. Name and describe the function of five of them.

Chapter 5
Airframe Nonmetallic Structures

ANALYSIS QUESTIONS

name:

date:

6. Describe the four steps in assessing the damage to composite materials.

7. What are some safety hazards associated with working with advanced composites and how can you mitigate them?

8. What transparent plastic materials are commonly used on aircraft? How do they differ from one another? What precautions should you take when handling them?

9. Describe the process of restoring a transparent plastic surface marred by a deep scratch.

10. What place does wooden construction hold in modern aircraft building? Why should you still know something about repairing wooden aircraft structures?

Chapter 6
Welding Techniques

FILL IN THE BLANK QUESTIONS

name:

date:

1. The two main types of fuselage trusses are the Pratt truss and the _____ .

2. Metal tubes that run from the firewall to the tail of an aircraft are called _____ .

3. A joint is where two tubes connect to each other; a _____ is where more than two tubes connect to each other.

4. When metal is _____ , it increases in length and breadth.

5. When metal cools, it _____ slightly more than it expanded when heated.

6. Normalizing temperature is _____ .

7. To show the temperature of the metal undergoing normalization, use a _____ .

8. _____ is a fusion process in which heat is supplying by burning a mixture of oxygen and acetylene. It is also known as _____ .

9. The flame temperature of an oxyacetylene torch is _____ to _____ .

10. The oxygen in a cylinder should never be brought in contact with _____ .

11. An acetylene tank is painted _____ .

12. The _____ is the unit used to mix oxygen and acetylene in the proper proportions and control the volume of the gases and the direction of the flame.

13. Oxygen hose fittings have _____ threads, and the nut is _____ .

14. To ignite a welding torch, use a _____ . Never use a _____ .

15. A _____ , in which an excess of acetylene is burned, is used when welding nickel alloys.

16. A _____ melts metal without changing its properties and leaves the metal clear and clean.

17. A _____ is a momentary backward flow of the gases at the torch tip that causes the flame to go out.

Chapter 6
Welding Techniques

FILL IN THE BLANK QUESTIONS

name:

date:

18. A _____ is the burning of gases within the torch. It is accompanied by a _____ sound or a _____ noise. Turn the gases off immediately.

19. Extinguish a welding flame by closing the _____ first, then closing the _____.

20. Whenever possible, weld in the _____ position.

21. A _____ is used for metals 1/16 to 1/8 inch thick.

22. A _____ is more commonly used in spot welding than in gas welding.

23. A _____ is formed when the edge or end of one piece of metal is welded to the surface of another.

24. Edge joints are usually made by bending the edges of one or both parts upward, placing the bend ends _____ to each other, and welding along the _____ formed by the edges.

25. If the edges of a long seam are placed in contact before welding starts, the far ends of the seam will _____ before the weld is completed.

26. When it is necessary to reweld a joint, all _____ must be removed before the new weld is begun.

27. As the _____ of steel increases, welding becomes more difficult.

28. Weldable carbon steels require no _____ and no _____. Adjust the torch flame to _____.

29. Only stainless steel that is used in _____ can be welded satisfactorily.

30. Aluminum plates _____ or thicker should be preheated in order to prevent cracks and to assure complete penetration. Warm them with the torch prior to welding.

31. Aluminum welding flux removes the _____ that might otherwise cause a defective weld.

32. Using _____ or _____ colored lenses allows the welder to see a change in the surface appearance of aluminum just before the metal melts.

33. A _____ combines a heating flame with a jet of pure oxygen under pressure.

Chapter 6
Welding Techniques

FILL IN THE BLANK QUESTIONS

name:

date:

34. Brazing involves joining metals using a non-ferrous bonding material with a melting point higher than _____ but lower than the metals being joined.

35. Examples of brazing include _____ soldering, _____ , and hard soldering.

36. Gas-tungsten arc welding is still known as _____ welding, while gas metal-arc welding is still known as _____ welding.

37. In gas tungsten-arc welding, an _____ is used to protect the weld zone from the atmosphere. _____ for the weld is provided by an intense electric arc struck between a tungsten electrode and the work.

38. In gas tungsten-arc welding, the _____ is not melted or used as filler material.

39. The inert gas used in gas tungsten-arc welding is _____ or _____ .

40. Gas metal-arc welding uses a _____ current and a gas shield of argon, helium, or carbon dioxide. A small-diameter wire serves as both _____ and filler metal.

41. _____ involves placing a pin onto the seam that is to be welded. The pin rotates as it travels down the seam and the friction _____ the aluminum.

Chapter 6
Welding Techniques

MULTIPLE CHOICE QUESTIONS

name:

date:

1. The use of welded steel tubing in aircraft construction was pioneered in 1910 by:
   a. Manfred von Richtofen
   b. Anton Hermann Gerhard Fokker
   c. Capt. von Steubing
   d. Orville and Wilbur Wright

2. The style of truss that includes cross-bracing borrowed from wooden bridge construction techniques is called:
   a. Warren truss
   b. Whitney truss
   c. Pratt truss
   d. Ingodwe truss

3. Which of these is not a characteristic of a good welded joint?
   a. Rigidity
   b. Low weight
   c. High strength
   d. Buckling

4. Which of these items is part of a portable oxyacetylene welding outfit?
   a. Direct current generator
   b. Oxygen and acetylene cylinders
   c. Tubing
   d. Both B and C

5. Ferrous filler material does not include:
   a. Carbon steel rods
   b. Alloy steel rods
   c. Aluminum rods
   d. Iron rods

6. A carburizing flame:
   a. Results from burning excess oxygen
   b. Results from burning excess acetylene
   c. Consists of two distinct zones
   d. Makes the weld six times as strong

7. A backfire may be caused by:
   a. Touching the tip to the work
   b. Overheating the tip
   c. Dirt in the end of the tip
   d. Any of these

8. If a flashback occurs, you should:
   a. Immediately turn off the gases
   b. Continue working, as it will go away soon
   c. Relight the torch as soon as possible
   d. Replace one of the metal pieces being welded

9. The technique in which filler rod is added to the puddle between the flame and the finished weld is called:
   a. Forehand welding
   b. Annealing
   c. Tungsten gas-arc welding
   d. Backhand welding

Chapter 6
Welding Techniques

MULTIPLE CHOICE QUESTIONS

name:

date:

10. When two pieces of metal are placed edge to edge with no overlap, and then welded, the resulting joint is called a:
    a. Butt joint
    b. Vertical weld
    c. Edge joint
    d. Double bevel

11. A tee joint joins:
    a. Two edges
    b. Three edges
    c. The edge of one piece and the surface of another
    d. Thick stock

12. The single-fillet and double-fillet are types of:
    a. Fish knives
    b. Corner joints
    c. Tee joints
    d. Lap joints

13. Chill bars are used to:
    a. Increase heat
    b. Absorb heat
    c. Obtain adult beverages
    d. Preheat metal that is about to be welded

14. Which of the following is not a characteristic of a completed, well-executed weld?
    a. The seam is smooth
    b. The joint is built up
    c. The weld tapers smoothly into the base metal
    d. Oxide build-up on the base metal close to the weld

15. To remove rust or scale from steel prior to welding:
    a. Dip the metal in a mixture of ammonium nitrate and water
    b. Run the metal through a commercial dishwasher
    c. Sandblast the piece and then remove the residue with a stainless steel brush
    d. Use a suitable grease solvent

16. When welding chrome-molybdenum steel, the area surrounding the weld must be preheated to:
    a. Between 200° and 300° F
    b. Between 300° and 400° F
    c. Between 1,000° and 1,100° F
    d. Between 100° and 250° F

17. On an aircraft, only weld stainless steel used for:
    a. Cooking utensils
    b. Structural components
    c. Nonstructural members
    d. Cockpit structures

18. One problem in welding aluminum is that the metal melts before:
    a. Before the surface oxide melts
    b. It is completely heated
    c. At a higher temperature than the surface oxide
    d. Only when flux is added

19. When welding aluminum, which rod should you use when maximum resistance to corrosion and high ductility are the most important concerns?
    a. 4043
    b. 5150
    c. 1492
    d. 1100

20. According to the table in Figure 4, to cut metal 2 inches thick with an oxyacetylene cutting torch, use tip number 2 and an oxygen pressure of:
    a. 40 pounds
    b. 50 pounds
    c. 60 pounds
    d. 70 pounds

APPROXIMATE PRESSURE FOR VARIOUS TIP SIZES			
Tip number	Thickness of Metal (in inches)	Acetylene Pressure (in pounds)	Oxygen Pressure (in pounds)
1	1/8	4	10
1	1/4	4	15
1	3/8	4	20
1	1/2	4	25
2	3/4	5	30
2	1	5	40
2	1 1/2	5	50
2	2	5	60
3	3	6	70
3	4	6	80
3	5	6	90
4	6	7	100
4	8	7	130
4	10	8	160

Figure 4.

21. If the oxyacetylene cutting torch moves too slowly:
    a. The flame may melt the edges of the cut
    b. The cutting jet will fail to go all the way through the material
    c. The oxygen lever will release
    d. The preheat orifice will conflict with the acetylene needle valve

22. What are two metals that can be cut with a plasma cutter but not with an oxyacetylene torch?
    a. Stainless steel and copper
    b. Aluminum and lead
    c. Aluminum and stainless steel
    d. Chromium and cesium

23. A plasma cutter cuts metal by using:
    a. An ionized airstream heated by high voltage
    b. Rotating steel blades
    c. A mixture of oxygen and acetylene
    d. Inert gases

24. Brazing includes which of the following techniques?
    a. Silver soldering
    b. Bronze welding
    c. Hard soldering
    d. All of these

25. The main use of silver soldering in aircraft maintenance is:
    a. Wing chord reduction
    b. Fabrication of high-pressure oxygen lines
    c. Creating edge joints
    d. None of these

Chapter 6
Welding Techniques

MULTIPLE CHOICE QUESTIONS

name:

date:

Chapter 6
Welding Techniques

MULTIPLE CHOICE QUESTIONS

name:

date:

26. In gas-shielded arc welding, a noncombustible gas is used to:
    a. Protect the welder from heat
    b. Shield the electrode, arc, molten metal weld, and weld area from the atmosphere
    c. Consume tungsten electrodes
    d. Make filler material unimportant

27. Where does the intense heat for gas tungsten-arc (TIG) welding come from?
    a. A flame between an electrode and the torch
    b. Friction between the atmosphere and the metal
    c. An electric arc struck between a tungsten electrode and the work
    d. A melted electrode

28. Which of these metals can be joined using TIG welding?
    a. Corrosion-resistant steel
    b. Magnesium
    c. Aluminum
    d. All of these

29. What gases are used in TIG welding?
    a. Helium
    b. Argon
    c. A and B
    d. None of these

30. Joining two pieces of aluminum with TIG welding:
    a. Does not require flux
    b. Requires flux
    c. Is not recommended
    d. Increases the strength of the metal

31. To break a TIG welding arc:
    a. Cut power to the welding unit
    b. Move the metal a safe distance from the torch
    c. Rapidly snap the electrode to a horizontal position
    d. Chill the electrode

32. Which of these types of stainless steel is used in aircraft construction?
    a. Austenitic
    b. Martensitic
    c. Ferritic
    d. Soporific

33. Gas metal-arc (MIG) welding uses:
    a. Direct current
    b. Alternating current
    c. A gas shield of argon, helium, or carbon dioxide
    d. A and C

34. One way that MIG welding differs from TIG welding is:
    a. The electrode is consumed during MIG welding
    b. MIG welding requires an electrical power source
    c. TIG welding uses a gas as to shield the work, while MIG welding does not
    d. MIG welding can be performed on aluminum

35. To break a MIG welding arc:
    a. Rapidly snap the electrode to a horizontal position
    b. Release the trigger
    c. Move the metal being welded
    d. Shut off the helium gas

Chapter 6
Welding Techniques

MULTIPLE CHOICE QUESTIONS

name:

date:

36. A properly established MIG welding arc:
    a. Has a loud, crackling sound
    b. Sounds like a siren
    c. Has a soft, sizzling sound
    d. Is about three inches long

37. Porous MIG welds can be caused by:
    a. Low arc voltage (less than 26 volts)
    b. Inadequate shielding gas flow
    c. Improperly cleaned base metal or dirty welding wire
    d. Any of these

38. Because both MIG and TIG welding utilize electrical current:
    a. The area being welded must be dry
    b. They work well in remote areas
    c. The torch can be rested on the workbench
    d. Protective clothing is not necessary

39. The advantages of friction stir welding include:
    a. Smoothness of the finished skin
    b. Corrosion resistance
    c. A and B
    d. None of these

40. If the method for inspecting a weld is not spelled out in an Airworthiness Directive or Operational Directive, what is the default method of inspection?
    a. Tapping the joint with a hammer
    b. Stress testing
    c. Visual inspection
    d. Core sampling

Chapter 6
Welding Techniques

ANALYSIS QUESTIONS

name:

date:

1. Describe what happens to metal as it is heated and then cooled.

2. Describe the equipment used in oxyacetylene welding.

3. Oxyacetylene welding flames are classified as neutral, carburizing, and oxidizing. What is each type of flame used for, and how is it obtained?

4. Describe the appearance of the three types of oxyacetylene welding flames. Which is the hottest?

5. How should the welding torch be held and used in oxyacetylene welding?

6. Describe how to weld a seam joining to pieces of sheet metal without having the pieces overlap each other at the end of the weld.

7. What are the characteristics of a finished, well-executed weld?

8. What are some things you should do to prepare metal for welding?

Chapter 6
Welding Techniques

9. Describe the procedure for cutting metal using an oxyacetylene torch.

ANALYSIS QUESTIONS

name:

date:

10. What is the function of the shielding gas in gas-shielded arc welding?

11. What are some disadvantages of gas tungsten-arc (TIG) welding?

12. List and briefly describe the equipment used in MIG welding.

13. Describe how to start and break the arc in MIG welding.

14. How is filler metal provided to a gas metal-arc (MIG) weld?

15. Describe how to run a MIG welding bead.

Chapter 7
Painting and Refinishing

FILL IN THE BLANK QUESTIONS

name:

date:

1. The primary objective of any aircraft paint finish is to protect exposed surfaces from _____ and other forms of deterioration.

2. The most popular base color for aircraft paint jobs is _____.

3. _____ is the repair of small areas where paint has been worn away or removed.

4. The effectiveness and adhesion of paint finish depends on careful _____.

5. After a control surface is refinished, it must be _____ by an A&P or certified repairman.

6. _____ involves firing a trajectory medium at a painted surface to remove the paint.

7. Removed paint is considered a _____, or HAZMAT, and must be properly disposed of.

8. Chemicals used to remove paint are called _____.

9. Prior to cleaning and stripping an aircraft, make sure it is _____ to dissipate the static electricity that may be generated.

10. A _____ of paint stripper may not be enough to loosen the paint.

11. Paint stripper takes _____ to _____ minutes to loosen paint, depending on the air temperature, humidity, and the condition of the paint.

12. You can perform a simple _____ test to check whether a surface is clean.

13. _____ is a simple chemical treatment for aluminum alloys that increases the metal's corrosion resistance and improves its paint bonding properties. It has all but replaced _____ in aircraft work.

14. Aged paint surfaces should be _____ to ensure the adhesion of overcoating paint.

15. To ensure a smooth transition between new paint and old paint, _____ the paint along the edge of an area that has been chemically stripped.

Chapter 7
Painting and Refinishing

FILL IN THE BLANK QUESTIONS

name:

date:

16. Epoxy-polymide primer comes in two separate components that must be mixed prior to use: the _____ , or color, in an epoxy vehicle, and a _____ used as a hardener for epoxy resin.

17. The viscosity of thinned epoxy-polymide primer can be checked using a _____ .

18. There are two types of _____ used on aircraft: aromatic and aliphatic.

19. Always wear _____ when mixing thinners and solvents.

20. The _____ type of polyurethane is the standard general-purpose exterior protective coating for aircraft.

21. A _____ is a painting defect where too much paint was applied and gravity caused the paint to drip down.

22. The painting defects known as fisheyes are often caused by the surface not having been _____ enough prior to painting.

23. _____ are the preferred topcoat material for aircraft markings and safety stripes.

24. Zinc chromate primer should only be used on the _____ of aircraft.

25. The process of covering surfaces that aren't supposed to receive paint is called _____ .

26. A _____ spray gun is designed for small paint jobs.

27. When a large area has to be painted, use a _____ spray gun.

28. When using a spray gun, hold the gun so that the spray is _____ to the area where the finish is being applied.

29. Hold a spray gun _____ inches from the work when spraying epoxy-polyamide or polyurethane; 8 to 10 inches away when applying lacquer; and _____ inches away for enamels.

30. Spray the primer, tack coat, and _____ in different directions.

31. Trim can be applied after the _____ has dried and the trim pattern has been masked.

32. FAR 45.29 explains what size _____ should be.

33. When you turn a spray gun's spreader adjustment dial to the right, a _____ pattern results. When you turn it to the left, a _____ pattern results.

34. If too much paint is being applied to the surface, turn the _____ on the spray gun to the right.

35. _____ uses electrostatic equipment to attract the paint to the work, but does not use _____. It is primarily used at large facilities to paint large airplanes.

36. Sealants can be used in an aircraft to maintain _____ in cabin areas, as well as for other purposes.

37. There are three types of sealants: _____, drying, and _____.

38. _____ are solids and are used around access panels and doors in areas where pressurization cavities must be maintained.

39. A drying sealant sets and cures as the _____ it is mixed with evaporates.

40. _____ are transformed from a fluid or semi-fluid state into a solid by a chemical reaction with a catalyst.

Chapter 7
Painting and Refinishing

FILL IN THE BLANK QUESTIONS

name:

date:

Chapter 7
Painting and Refinishing

MULTIPLE CHOICE QUESTIONS

name:

date:

1. Touch-up painting involves the application of two materials. They are:
   a. Primer and secondary
   b. Primer and a compatible topcoat
   c. Lacquer and vinyl
   d. Primer and aromatic-type polyurethane

2. Since it is hard to match older aircraft paint exactly, touch-up jobs usually involve:
   a. Redoing an entire side of the aircraft
   b. Redoing the nosecone in addition to the spot that needs repair
   c. Redoing the finish on a complete section or surface
   d. Waiting until a bigger area needs to be repainted

3. What documentation can you consult to find a list of cleaning materials acceptable for use on a given aircraft?
   a. Aircraft Maintenance Manual
   b. SRM
   c. Aircraft Cleaning: Yesterday, Today, and Tomorrow
   d. A HAZMAT manual

4. Which of the following are used to strip paint by media blasting?
   a. Rice hulls
   b. Walnut shells
   c. Dry ice crystals
   d. All of these

5. Media reclamation:
   a. Reclaims or collects used media and the material it removes
   b. Sorts old paint by color
   c. Involves the reuse of stripped paint
   d. Is part of any chemical paint stripping process

6. What should be done to surfaces that can be harmed by a paint stripper prior to applying the stripper?
   a. Those parts should be removed from the airplane
   b. They should be masked
   c. There are no such surfaces if you use the correct chemical
   d. Sealant should be applied to them

7. If stripping must be done in a hangar, make sure that there is adequate:
   a. Distance between aircraft
   b. Surface area inside the hangar
   c. Ventilation
   d. Tools

8. When working on stripping small sections, use a fiber brush and cover the area with the stripper to a depth of:
   a. 1/2 inch
   b. 1/128 to 1/64 inch
   c. 1/32 to 1/16 inch
   d. 1/8 to 1/4 inch

9. What process helps primer adhere better to aluminum?
   a. Anodizing
   b. Scuff-sanding
   c. Zahn testing
   d. Alodizing

Chapter 7
Painting and Refinishing

MULTIPLE CHOICE QUESTIONS

name:

date:

10. The areas of old paint next to the area that is being touched-up with new paint should be:
    a. Anodized
    b. Treated with pliable sealant
    c. Scuff-sanded
    d. Suction fed

11. If the two components of epoxy-polyamide primer are not mixed in the ratio recommended by the manufacturer, what can be the result?
    a. Poor adhesion of the material to the surface
    b. Poor chemical resistance
    c. A and B
    d. None of these

12. In order to apply epoxy-polyamide primer with a spray gun, it must be thinned, stirred thoroughly, strained, and:
    a. Stirred again
    b. Allowed to stand for 15 minutes
    c. Mixed with additional parts of the pigment
    d. Applied immediately

13. If epoxy-polyamide primer is correctly thinned, how long will it take to drain out of a No. 2 Zahn cup?
    a. 17 to 18 seconds
    b. Most of the day
    c. 20 seconds
    d. 10 to 12 seconds

14. The aromatic type of polyurethane is used in what type of coatings?
    a. Cured
    b. General-purpose exterior
    c. Rain erosion-resistant
    d. Alodized

15. The aliphatic type of polyurethane is used in what type of coatings?
    a. Cured
    b. General-purpose exterior
    c. Rain erosion-resistant
    d. Anodized

16. Which of these statements about aliphatic-type polyurethane is not true?
    a. It is used over epoxy-polyamide primer.
    b. Its two components—pigmented material and catalyst—must be mixed prior to use.
    c. It can be used for touch-up over other polyurethane systems.
    d. It was previously used on almost all aircraft, but now is only rarely used.

17. A painting defect in which paint on an entire panel moves down at the same time is called:
    a. A run
    b. A sag
    c. An orange peel
    d. Wrinkling

18. Not using cross-coats or not overlapping them enough can cause:
    a. Light and dark streaks
    b. Orange peel
    c. Runs
    d. Fisheyes

Chapter 7
Painting and Refinishing

MULTIPLE CHOICE QUESTIONS

name:

date:

19. Within how many hours after primer application should polyurethane paint be applied?
    a. 12 hours
    b. 24 hours
    c. 8 hours
    d. 3 hours

20. What is the preferred topcoat material for touching up avionic components and instruments?
    a. Aromatic-type polyurethane
    b. Zinc-chromate primer
    c. Acrylic nitrocellulose lacquer
    d. Enamel

21. What do you use to thin zinc chromate primer?
    a. Mineral spirits
    b. Turpentine
    c. Water
    d. Zoluol

22. What activities should you not allow in areas where paint or solvent is being used?
    a. Eating
    b. Drinking
    c. Smoking
    d. All of these

23. In areas where the colored paint being applied will leave a clean line, what masking material is recommended?
    a. Fine-line tape
    b. Plastic sheeting
    c. No masking is required if the spray gun is properly handled
    d. Trim-line tape

24. Which type of spray gun is designed for small jobs?
    a. Pressure-feed
    b. Atomizing
    c. Fluid-feed
    d. Suction-feed

25. Which of the following can introduce air into the fluid line of a spray gun?
    a. A clogged air vent
    b. Lack of material in the cup
    c. An obstructed fluid passage
    d. A loose packing nut

26. Hobby-type paint guns:
    a. Are acceptable for even an expensive refinishing job
    b. Generally produce unacceptable finishes
    c. Are an inexpensive version of a pressure-feed spray gun
    d. Have been banned by the FAA

27. When painting the corner of a piece with a spray gun, the gun should be directed:
    a. First to one side, then the other
    b. To the surface on the operator's right
    c. Directly at the corner, so that the paint hits both sides of the corner equally
    d. Downward and directly at the corner

Chapter 7
Painting and Refinishing

MULTIPLE CHOICE QUESTIONS

name:

date:

28. "Triggering" a spray gun in order to avoid an uneven coat at the beginning and end of a stroke means:
    a. That the spray gun is stationary when the spray is activated
    b. That the spray gun trigger is pulsed rapidly during the stroke
    c. That the air compressor is temporarily deactivated
    d. Starting the gun toward the area to be sprayed before depressing the trigger, and keeping the gun moving after the trigger has been released

29. In parallel passes with a spray gun, the two applications of paint should overlap by:
    a. About 50%
    b. About 1 inch
    c. About 25%
    d. As little as possible

30. In painting trim, what is the general order in which the colors are applied?
    a. Red, orange, yellow, green, blue, indigo, and violet
    b. Lightest color first, followed by the next-darkest color
    c. Darkest color first, followed by the next-lightest color
    d. It depends on the type of paint rather than color

31. Excessive fluid pressure during spray painting can lead to:
    a. Dusting and rippling of the finish
    b. Runs in the finish
    c. Orange peel and sags in the finish
    d. Curing

32. Which of these is not a type of sealant?
    a. Rising
    b. Curing
    c. Drying
    d. Pliable

33. Sealant should not be applied to metal that is colder than:
    a. 85° F
    b. 60° F
    c. 32° F
    d. 70° F

34. Which of these will prevent an effective seal after sealant is applied?
    a. Air bubbles
    b. A continuous bead
    c. Spraying on the sealant
    d. Injection guns

35. What documentation can you look in to find information on the recommended method for pressure-sealing the joints and seams of an aircraft?
    a. Sealant manufacturer's information
    b. SRM
    c. FAA Directive 42
    d. General Aircraft Seam Maintenance in the Twenty-First Century, 2nd edition

36. Spreading sealant along a seam with a sealant injection gun is called:
    a. Fillet-sealing
    b. Curing sealing
    c. Sealing compounds
    d. De-icing

Chapter 7
Painting and Refinishing

ANALYSIS QUESTIONS

name:

date:

1. What are some paints commonly used on aircraft?

2. What are some reasons to repaint an aircraft?

3. Why is white the most popular base color for aircraft?

4. Give a general description of how you would go about stripping paint from an aircraft.

5. Describe how you perform a water break test. What does such a test indicate?

6. What should you do if the material you are thinning drains from a Zahn cup more slowly than it should? What about if it drains too quickly?

7. What are the two main types of polyurethane paint systems, and how are they used on aircraft?

8. List four types of paint defects and their respective causes.

9. Where are some places on an aircraft that you would use zinc chromate primer? Where would you avoid using it?

Chapter 7
Painting and Refinishing

ANALYSIS QUESTIONS

name:

date:

10. Describe how you would clean a pressure-feed spray gun.

11. What would be the benefits of an effectively designed sequence for applying paint to an aircraft? Can you think of such a sequence?

12. Describe how paints, strippers, thinners, and similar substances should be stored. What should be done with flammable waste from a painting operation?

13. How is a curing sealant different from a drying sealant?

14. Describe the process of fillet-sealing.

15. Describe the process of injection-sealing.

Chapter 8
Assembly and Rigging

FILL IN THE BLANK QUESTIONS

name:

date:

1. In addition to the information provided in aircraft maintenance manuals and aircraft specifications, _____ also provide information regarding control surface travel.

2. _____ is the tendency of an object to remain stationary when supported at its own center of gravity.

3. A flight control surface which has too much weight behind the center of gravity is said to be _____ .

4. A control surface, where all rotating forces are balanced and there is no vibration, is said to be _____ balanced.

5. Better flight operations are gained from flight controls that are _____ or _____ .

6. Flight control balance is often achieved by the use of _____ .

7. Control surface counterbalance weights are often made from _____ or from _____ .

8. In addition to the direct cables to the ailerons there is also a _____ cable.

9. The rigging for most ailerons involves rigging the ailerons to the _____ position.

10. The simplest wing flaps are _____ operated by the use of _____ or _____ .

11. A moving horizontal stabilizer on a cantilevered tail is referred to as a _____ .

12. A _____ tail on a modern aircraft has is bolted and typically has no adjustments.

13. Stiff control cable that is not suitable for making turns is _____ cable, while the most easily bent cable is referred to as _____ cable.

14. Steel cable that is _____ is preferred when the weather and outside elements are a factor in cable life, but it is not as strong as _____ cable.

15. The Nicopress process uses _____ to create a loop of cable and an eye that can hold the full rated strength of the cable.

16. When making a _____ , two copper sleeves are used to connect two pieces of cable together.

Chapter 8
Assembly and Rigging

FILL IN THE BLANK QUESTIONS

name:

date:

17. The length of a copper sleeve on a 3/32 inch cable before the swaging compression is _____ long, and after the swaging compression the copper sleeve is _____ long.

18. _____ terminals are suitable for use in civil aircraft up to and including maximum cable loads.

19. Areas in the aircraft such as _____ , _____ , and lavatories are prime areas where aircraft control cables tend to corrode.

20. Control rods are used as links in a control system and give a _____ motion.

21. Rod bearings come in _____ and _____ type configurations.

22. If a rod is _____ it cannot be repaired and is no longer airworthy.

23. A _____ is used in the cable system to adjust cable tension.

24. _____ or a _____ are both acceptable means of securing a turnbuckle.

25. The means for leveling an aircraft can be found in _____ .

26. While wing dihedral and wing incidence are not adjustable on most aircraft, these should be checked in the event of a _____ , or if the aircraft has experienced _____ .

27. Fiber or nylon locking nuts should not be used in areas where the temperature can be expected to exceed _____ °F.

28. _____ (0.020 inch diameter) should be used to seal equipment such as first-aid kits, portable fire extinguishers, emergency valves, or oxygen regulators.

Chapter 8
Assembly and Rigging

MULTIPLE CHOICE QUESTIONS

name:

date:

1. Which of the following areas in the Type Certificate Data Sheet are of primary interest with respect to rigging an aircraft?
   a. Control surface travel limits
   b. Datum location
   c. Weight and balance information
   d. Aircraft performance and limitations data

2. In addition to the Type Certificate Data Sheets what other document or publication is required for properly assembling and rigging an aircraft?
   a. The AC 43.13
   b. Title 14 CFR 43
   c. The approved manufacturer's maintenance manual
   d. An FAA for 337 Major Repair or Alteration Form

3. An out-of-balance condition in a flight control surface shows up as which of the following problems?
   a. Control surface flutter that can damage the aircraft
   b. The flight controls will be difficult to move by the pilot
   c. The control surfaces will not deflect to their proper angles
   d. The weight and balance of the aircraft will not fall within the published center of gravity limits

4. Which of the following control surface balance conditions is generally preferred by the aircraft manufacturers?
   a. Overbalanced
   b. Underbalanced
   c. Perfectly balanced
   d. Laterally balanced

5. Which of the following is NOT a method of balancing a flight control?
   a. Dynamic method
   b. Calculation method
   c. Scale method
   d. Balance beam method

6. Where are control surface counterbalance weights located?
   a. At the control surface center of gravity
   b. On the trailing edges of the flight control
   c. On the leading edges of the flight control or in front of the hinge line
   d. On the hinge point of the flight control

7. Which of the following devices are used to measure control surface travel?
   a. A bubble protractor
   b. A propeller protractor
   c. A laser level
   d. All of the above

8. Which flight control should be adjusted, or have its position verified, before working on the aileron system?
   a. The trailing edge wing flaps
   b. The rudders
   c. The elevators
   d. The trim tabs

9. With the control columns locked at neutral, how is the neutral position of the ailerons usually determined?
   a. By setting the upper aileron surface to a position specified in the Type Certificate Data Sheet
   b. By adjusting the balance cable to the tension specified in the maintenance manual
   c. By aligning the trailing edge of the ailerons with the trailing edge of the flaps
   d. By using an aileron position tool

Chapter 8
Assembly and Rigging

MULTIPLE CHOICE QUESTIONS

name:

date:

10. What final action should be taken when rigging the flight controls?
    a. Make sure that the control surfaces travel in the proper direction and by the proper amount
    b. Set the cable tension on the balance cable
    c. Check the neutral position of the control surface
    d. Verify that the flight control falls within the balance limits specified in the aircraft maintenance manual

11. A control cable that is designated as a 7x19 would have what kind of construction?
    a. 19 layers or bundles of wires with each bundle containing 7 individual strands of wire
    b. Seven layers or bundles of wires with each bundle containing 19 individual strands of wire
    c. Seven wires twisted 19 times per inch in a counterclockwise direction
    d. 7/32 in diameter with 19 individual bundles or layers of wire

12. Which of the following cable sizes would be considered to be the most easily bent and the best for making turns around pulleys?
    a. 1 x 1
    b. 7 x 19
    c. 7 x 1
    d. 7 x 7

13. Which of the following cause aircraft control cables to wear, become brittle, and break?
    a. Bending around pulleys
    b. Friction from dirt or sand on the cables
    c. Vibration of the cables on long straight runs
    d. All of the above

14. A swaged on control cable end is expected to be how strong as compared to the cable's maximum rated breaking strength?
    a. The swaged end should carry 100% of the cable's full-rated breaking strength
    b. The swaged end should carry 95% of the cable's rated breaking strength
    c. The swaged end should carry 80% of the cable's rated breaking strength
    d. The swaged end should carry 70% of the cable's rated breaking strength

15. The smallest size cable that should be used on a primary flight control surface is which of the following?
    a. 1/16 inch
    b. 1/8 inch
    c. 5/32 inch
    d. ¼ inch

16. How should swage type terminal ends be checked for proper shank diameter after swaging?
    a. Telescoping gage
    b. Go No-Go gauge
    c. Micrometer
    d. Both B and C above

17. After assembling a cable end onto an aircraft control cable the cable should be proof loaded to what value?
    a. 90% of the cable's rated breaking strength
    b. 70% of the cable's rated breaking strength
    c. 60% of the cable's rated breaking strength
    d. 50% of the cable's rated breaking strength

18. Cable rigging charts compensate for which of the following conditions?
    a. Different cable diameters
    b. Different temperatures
    c. Different cable lengths
    d. The number of pulleys the cable must go around

Chapter 8
Assembly and Rigging

MULTIPLE CHOICE QUESTIONS

name:

date:

19. On many aircraft the rigging of controls is simplified by the use of:
    a. Digital protractors
    b. Jigs and alignment fixtures
    c. Rigging pins
    d. All of the above

20. Replacable bearings in the ends of push-pull rods are retained in the push-pull rod end by means of:
    a. Normal press fit
    b. Normal press fit with staking
    c. Normal press fit with a chemical retaining compound such as Locktite®
    d. All of the above.

21. Sealed ball bearing rod ends should be cleaned using which of the following methods?
    a. Spray them off with a high pressure water washer or spray gun
    b. Rinse them completely using a light spray of mineral spirits or degreasing solvent
    c. Wipe them off with a rag
    d. All of the above

22. What are the maximum number of threads that are allowed to be exposed outside of a turnbuckle?
    a. 4
    b. 3
    c. 2
    d. 1

23. Using the grid method or placing a spirit level across pegs in the aircraft represent two methods of:
    a. Measuring the flight control surface travel
    b. Measuring the alignment of the aircraft structure
    c. Measuring to see if the aircraft is level
    d. None of the above

24. What is the reason for checking wing dihedral angle and wing incidence angle in most modern aircraft?
    a. To make sure the aircraft has not been distorted by high G loads, extreme turbulence, or hard landings
    b. To determine how much control surface travel is allowed for an aircraft
    c. All aircraft require wing dihedral and wing adjustments in order to make the aircraft fly straight and level
    d. To set the proper control cable tension

25. When are self locking nuts not allowed to be used?
    a. Where the parts they connect subject the bolt and nut to rotational forces
    b. On panels or doors that are frequently disassembled before or after flight
    c. Anywhere that the nut may fall off inside or be drawn into a turbine engine inlet
    d. Any of the above

26. The application and temperature environment recommended for a self-locking nut can be determined by which of the following methods?
    a. The AN or MS number stamped on the nut
    b. The finish material on the nut
    c. Title 14CFR Part 43
    d. All of the above

Chapter 8
Assembly and Rigging

MULTIPLE CHOICE QUESTIONS

name:

date:

27. What size stainless steel safety wire should be used when performing the single wire method?
    a. 0.020
    b. 0.032
    c. 0.041
    d. The largest wire that will fit in the hole of the bolt or nut

28. Which of the following is true regarding putting safety wire on a bolt or nut?
    a. Attach the safety wire so the wire will pull the nut or bolt in the tightening direction
    b. Do not use wire that has been previously twisted, always use new wire
    c. The wire must be tight enough not to vibrate, but not so tight that the wire may break
    d. All of the above

Chapter 8
Assembly and Rigging

ANALYSIS QUESTIONS

name:

date:

1. Why are transport category aircraft more difficult to disassemble and reassemble?

2. Why is it important to consult the aircraft maintenance manual or the structural repair manual before removal or assembly of an aircraft structure?

3. Why must a movable flight control surface be balanced?

4. What is the difference between static balance and dynamic balance?

5. Counterbalance weights made from depleted uranium can be dangerous. What safety precautions should be taken regarding counterbalance weights made of this material?

6. Why is there more wear on aircraft control cables where the cable goes around pulleys?

7. What is the purpose of a nylon jacket on a control cable?

8. What is the copper oval sleeve stock number that is to be used on a 3/32 stainless steel control cable?

Chapter 8
Assembly and Rigging

ANALYSIS QUESTIONS

name:

date:

9. What is the procedure for making sure that a swage-type terminal does not slip on the cable during the swaging process, resulting in insufficient cable inside the terminal to sustain the cable loads?

10. Explain how to prevent bearings fitted into control rod ends from becoming dislodged or disconnected from the push pull rod.

11. Explain how to check an aircraft for proper wing dihedral.

12. What is the 3-4-5 method of measuring a 90° angle?

13. The rigging of an aircraft control system nearly always follows what three basic steps?

14. What is the final thing that should be done to a flight control system after the rigging is done?

Corrections, Suggestions for Improvement, Request for Additional Information

It is Avotek's goal to provide quality aviation maintenance resources to help you succeed in your career, and we appreciate your assistance in helping.

Please complete the following information to report a correction, suggestion for improvement, or to request additional information.

REFERENCE NUMBER (*To be assigned by Avotek*)	
CONTACT INFORMATION*	
Date	
Name	
Email	
Daytime Phone	
BOOK INFORMATION	
Title	
Edition	
Page number	
Figure/Table Number	
Discrepancy/Correction (*You may also attach a copy of the discrepancy/correction*)	
Suggestion(s) for Improvement (*Attach additional documentation as needed*)	
Request for Additional Information	
FOR AVOTEK USE ONLY	Date Received	
	Reference Number Issued By	
	Receipt Notification Sent	
	Action Taken/By	
	Completed Notification Sent	

*Contact information will only be used to provide updates to your submission or if there is a question regarding your submission.

Send your corrections to:

Email: comments@avotek.com
Fax: 1-540-234-9399
Mail: Corrections: Avotek Information Resources
P.O. Box 219
Weyers Cave, VA 24486 USA